Rich   218-77; W9-ADW-018

Bitter Herbs - p. 39
Passover

P. 17 extremely important
Every nation needs a great
leader - or it turns into
anarchy + tyranny!

From Blood p. 71 - 72

6:00 pm is the 1st Hour
of the night.
9:00 pm is the 3rd Hour
of the night.

ORIGEN of alexandria - the
Great christian Thinker
      p. 161

THE WORLD OF SAINT PAUL

JOSEPH M. CALLEWAERT

THE WORLD
OF
SAINT PAUL

Translated by Michael J. Miller

IGNATIUS PRESS   SAN FRANCISCO

Original French text:
L'Univers de l'Apôtre Paul

Cover image: *The Apostle Paul*
Impogeo degli Aurelii, Rome, Italy
Photograph by G. Dagli Orti
© DeA Picture Library/Art Resource

Cover design by Roxanne Mei Lum

Maps by David Notley
Camway Creative Limited

© 2011 by Ignatius Press, San Francisco
All rights reserved
ISBN 978-1-58617-412-5
Library of Congress Control Number 2010931313
Printed in the United States of America ⊗

To my brother,
Fr. Lucien Callewaert, C.Ss.R.
Sacerdos Sanctae Ecclesiae fidelissimus

Contents

Maps   9

Preface   11

1. In These Last Days   13

2. Saul of Tarsus   22

3. A Rabbinical Education   32

4. Metanoia, or the Conversion of Saul   42

5. The First Missionary Journey: Cyprus,
   Antioch of Pisidia, Iconium, Lystra and Derbe   56

6. The Second Missionary Journey I: Philippi,
   Thessalonica, Beroea   75

7. The Second Missionary Journey II: Athens
   and Corinth   92

8. The Third Missionary Journey   116

9. The Ascent to Jerusalem   130

10. Arrest and Imprisonment in Caesarea   145

11. Voyage to Rome: Crossing and Shipwreck   162

12. Paul Imprisoned in Rome   178

13. Final Journeys, Second Captivity, Martyrdom   187

Chronology of the Life of Saint Paul   203

Bibliography   207

MAPS

1. Antioch (in Syria)   51

2. The First Missionary Journey   57

3. The Second Missionary Journey   77

4. Corinth and Surrounding Area   109

5. Ephesus and Surrounding Area   118

6. The Third Missionary Journey   123

7. Final Stage of the Journey to Rome   171

9

Preface

> He [Saint Paul] is a chosen instrument of mine
> to carry my name before the Gentiles and kings
> and the sons of Israel; for I will show him how
> much he has to suffer for the sake of my name.
> —(Acts 9:15–16)

This book began in my mind on a beautiful Italian day, a
few years ago, as I was visiting the Basilica of San Paolo
fuori le Mura, that imposing church "outside the walls"
of Rome, so charged with memory. It stands on the Via
Ostiense and holds the body of Saint Paul, which the
emperor Constantine, early in the fourth century A.D.,
encased in a double sarcophagus of marble and bronze. It
was here, as I was contemplating the beautiful canopy of
Arnoldo di Cambio (1285) under which rests the apostle,
that I began reflecting how little average Christians know
about Saint Paul and his times. Realizing that few books
offer a style and a format accessible to them, I decided to
write just such a book.

This biography of Saint Paul is addressed to a main-
stream audience of Catholics and Christians as well as other
people of good will, who want to walk with a man who
was totally available to the guidance of the Holy Spirit in
his missionary journeys through the Greco-Roman world.

Across the East Mediterranean, the reader will follow
the apostle closely: in the heart of the Syrian desert; on the
high plateaus of arid Anatolia; in the Riviera of Pamphylia;
along the coast of Cyprus; sailing around the jagged islands
of the sun-drenched Aegean and Ionian seas; in the fertile
plains of Macedonia; up the tormented coastline of Achaia.

Everywhere they will listen to or read the gospel, always new, that the apostle Paul came to announce to the Jews and the Gentiles, in the synagogues and public places, two thousand years ago.

In my interpretation of Saint Paul, I have tried to absorb the spirit of his epoch as far as I could, and I put less trust in the present-day judgments, however brilliantly and learnedly expressed, than in the abiding traditions of the ages. If perhaps I have evoked a little too much history and pursued rather too long a road in regions so rich with a past, I have always made sure to trace a path that brings us back to this intrepid and tenacious Jew who will steadily appear in stark relief.

I have passed through the pale antechambers of "research" guided by reason and conscience, but well aware that each one of us, even an historian or exegete, is enveloped in the fashion of his times and his temperament. There is nothing in all this for humble people to fear, as if failure to accept the latest result of "biblical criticism" should immediately class one as an ignoramus. There is the authority of scholarship and there is also the authority of tradition, based on information accessible to us and sanctioned by the Church.

Of the authorities (one must have "Authorities") by whose lights in varying degrees I have been guided, I give a list in appendix. It is not as exhaustive as I wish, for it would fill another hundred pages, so rich and numerous are the bibliographic sources dealing with the apostle.

Before the invention of the printing press, when an exhausted scribe finished copying the Holy Bible or a treasured book or a valuable document, he exclaimed: *Deo gratias!* Saint Paul, however, gave me cause for thanksgiving from the start: writing this book began in a glow of pleasure, continued and ended with great delight.

Deo Gratias!

I

In These Last Days

Before entering upon the life of Saint Paul, let us consider how in his era the world had become a field well-suited to receiving and propagating the good news, the *euangelion*, of Jesus Christ. "In many and various ways God spoke of old to our fathers by the prophets; but *in these last days* he has spoken to us by a Son, whom he appointed the heir of all things, through whom also he created the ages" (Heb 1:1–2; italics added). And this Son, the Christ, commanded his disciples: "[Go].... And you shall be my witnesses in Jerusalem and in all Judea and Samaria and to the end of the earth" (Acts 1:8).

The world of the first century of our era had been prepared providentially to receive this gospel as a result of several favorable circumstances, which we will review quickly.

The Diaspora of the Jews

By 721 B.C. Sargon II of Assyria had taken more than twenty-seven thousand inhabitants of Samaria away in captivity to Asshur. At the same time a large number of Israelites from the same region took refuge in Egypt (see Hos 9:6).

Nearly one and a half centuries later, in June to July 587, Jerusalem was captured, the Temple was destroyed by Nebuchadnezzar, and a new deportation ensued. This caused a new influx of refugees in the land of the Nile, bringing with it the prophet Jeremiah, against his will.

Following the conquests of Alexander the Great, Greek became the lingua franca of almost the entire ancient East. The books of the Old Testament were translated into Greek, the Septuagint (LXX), for the benefit of the Hellenized Jews of Alexandria in Egypt. In 233 B.C., Antiochus IV Epiphanes colonized the entire coast of Asia Minor with émigrés, most of them Jewish, who were originally from Babylon and Palestine.

In 63 B.C. Pompey, the famous Roman general, brought some Jews as captives to Rome. Later these Romanized Jews provided Julius Caesar with funds to help him in his rise to power. In return, in 47 B.C. Caesar promulgated a decree worded as follows: "Hyrcanus and his sons will preserve all their rights to the title of high priest, whether it be granted to them by law or by a free gift. If, subsequently, a question arises concerning Jewish polity, I desire that it be settled by referring it to him." The decree continues: "All other measures notwithstanding, I allow these persons [the Jews] to gather and to organize their community following the customs of their fathers and according to their own laws." This favorable decree of Julius Caesar was approved after his death by the Senate of the Republic and later by Caesar Augustus also.

The historian and geographer Strabo reports that Jews inhabited all the cities of the ancient world and that it was not easy to find a place in the world where their influence was not felt. In his *Oratio pro Flacco*, Cicero speaks about thousands of Jews residing, around one century before Jesus Christ, in the province of Asia. This comprised the western part of present-day Turkey: Mysia, Lydia, Caria, and Phrygia. Herod Agrippa I wrote to the emperor Caligula,

"Jerusalem is the capital not only of Judaea but also of many other countries." The Jewish philosopher Philo of Alexandria, perhaps exaggerating somewhat, declared that more than a million Jews lived in Egypt. At the time of Paul, Jews in Rome numbered several thousands, served by numerous synagogues.

Some of these Israelites were well-to-do and even very rich. There were more than seventy gilded seats in the leading synagogue of Alexandria. Many synagogues were among the most beautiful buildings in Antioch and Alexandria. Mithridates Eupator, king of Pontus (112–62 B.C.), seized the Jewish treasury on the island of Cos, the value of which had been estimated at more than eight hundred talents, a considerable sum at the time. Flaccus, in the province of Asia, appropriated large sums destined for the Temple of Jerusalem. The commerce in grain produced in Egypt and shipped to Rome was largely in the hands of the Jews.

The Roman poet Juvenal notes that some Roman men had themselves circumcised and practiced the Jewish religion, following the Law handed down by Moses. Dio Cassius mentions, as an item of great interest, the expansion of Israel's religion throughout the empire. A high-ranking Roman noblewoman, Fulvia, sent some very precious gifts of purple and gold to the Temple in Jerusalem. For her part Poppaea Sabina, the mistress and later the wife of Nero, converted to Judaism.

These examples did not prevent the cultivated classes in Rome from hating the Jews. Cicero described their religion as "barbarous superstition". Juvenal ridiculed their refusal to eat pork. Tacitus treated "that abominable race" as sluggards, because they did not work on the Sabbath day or during the sabbatical year. But the Jewish historian Flavius Josephus retorted: "For a long time now, there has been great zeal among the masses for our religion; there is scarcely a Greek or barbarian city or nation in which the custom of resting on the seventh day is not observed." This is confirmed by Seneca, who writes, "This custom of that despised race is so widespread that it has been adopted in practice in all countries: the conquered have imposed their law on the conquerors."

The ground, therefore, had been prepared well. The Law was the *didaskalos* (teacher) who led the people to the Messiah, the Christ announced by the prophets. It would be the task of the apostles and especially of Paul to proclaim him to the ends of the earth.

Alexander the Great and the Roman Empire

The conquests of Alexander the Great also prepared for the spread of Christianity. Alexander's ambition was to gather all the nations and to make of them one unified world. He succeeded so well that Greek became the common language, the *koiné*, all around the Mediterranean, as far as Marseilles and the Pillars of Hercules.

Plutarch, a resident of Rome, did not speak Latin; nevertheless he had no difficulty discussing philosophy or becoming involved in politics. The letters of Paul were written in Greek just like the rest of the New Testament. A certain number of satirical graffiti, scratched on the walls of Rome during the time of Nero, were composed in Greek. Saint Jerome, in the fourth century, tells us that all of the Middle East spoke Greek. The Christian missionaries could express themselves in this language wherever the Spirit led them without having to worry about learning the language of the region that they were visiting.

The strategically located cities of Corinth, Carthage, and Numantia were destroyed. Roman rule extended over all the countries surrounding the Mediterranean.

But Rome could no longer remain the rugged, poor city of olden times. The ancient virtues yielded to the desire for rapid conquests. The people, whose sobriety and tenacity conquered the world and compelled its admiration, passed too quickly from the poverty that gave it its strength to the most immoderate opulence. "After the conquest of Macedonia," says Titus Livius (Livy), "[the Romans] thought that they could enjoy the universal empire and its spoils in complete security."

The conquest of Hellas with its works of art contributed to the spread of the general taste for luxury. The subjugation of Asia, which brought to Rome all the ostentation of the Orient, revealed to her an opulence that until then she had not even imagined, and dealt the final blow to her morals.

On the other hand, as a result of her victories, Rome was now the meeting place for the most diverse peoples. Travelers flocked there to dissipate their fortunes, enjoying in exchange all sorts of pleasures. We must mention also the legionaries who, after several campaigns, returned to Rome enriched and corrupted, in any case enemies now of work and eager for pleasures. They swelled the throng of commoners from all over Italy, for nowhere but in Rome was wheat distributed free of charge.

When a nation has arrived at the pinnacle of her power, when she is the mistress of the world, certain ambitions know no limit, placing her institutions at risk. She is at the mercy of a rebel or a lucky soldier. If she does not then find a man who places the future of the fatherland ahead of partisanship, there will be anarchy and tyranny.

What happened next is known by all: Antony and Cleopatra; the victory of Octavius at Actium; the destruction of the Republic; finally the accession to power of Octavius, who was proclaimed emperor under the name

of Augustus. Rome had decided that it was time, for the
sake of her future, to place her destiny in the steady hands
of a man who finally put an end to political anarchy and
brought peace to the Roman world, thus inaugurating an
era of tranquility.

This succession to the throne was an important factor
in the propagation of Christianity. During his reign (31
B.C. to A.D. 14), the empire included practically the whole
civilized world. Rome, a noisy city of luxury and servitude,
had truly become the capital of the world. Her influence
dazzled the entire known world, and the Barbarians themselves had their eyes stubbornly fixed on her.

All roads led to Rome, and those well-paved highways,
as well as the maritime trade routes, were rid of bandits
or pirates. The *Pax Romana*, a relative peace, of course,
reigned throughout the world.

Decadence of the Pagan Religion

The ingenious naïveté of the Mediterranean peoples had
been pleased to populate the invisible realm with a multitude of gods and goddesses in human form who were
distinguished from mere mortals only by their power and
their eternity.

Among the Greeks, this religion was based on the poems
of Homer and even of Hesiod, which were considered to
be quasi-sacred. Already in the third century before Christ,
however, Xenophon ridiculed the popular religion: "Homer
and Hesiod imputed everything under heaven to the gods."

Greedy, sensual, and jealous thieves and vindictive
scoundrels: these were gods of arbitrary pleasure with no
morality whatsoever. The stories about them do not lift
up the heart or calm the anxiety of mystery, nor do they
inspire a desire for the good.

The ancients were content to offer a purely formalistic worship to the hidden powers that move the world—provided that the ceremonies were conducted with the prescribed pomp and pageantry. Moreover this pagan religion was protected and supported by the state or the local authorities, who decided which gods should be venerated and to whom sacrifices could be offered.

The great gods of the official religion in Rome, *dii consentes*, were twelve in number: Jupiter, the king; Juno, his wife; Minerva, goddess of wisdom; Vulcan and Vesta, the god and goddess of fire; Ceres, goddess of the harvest; Neptune, god of the sea; Venus, goddess of love and beauty; Mars, god of war; Mercury, god of eloquence and commerce; Apollo, god of poetry and music; and Diana, goddess of festivals and hunting.

Uneasiness about Salvation

True religious piety had disappeared; nothing remained but an empty, idolatrous cult: a mixture of external, superstitious ritual and magic that did not satisfy the desire for an assurance of happiness, thanks to the protection of higher powers. Pessimism reigned. The poet Catullus, a contemporary of Virgil, lamented: "Once the ephemeral flame of our life is extinguished, we must sleep an eternal sleep." Everyone knew that everything ends badly, that nothing can be done to resist the stream that flows turbulently and ceaselessly until the end of time, but instead each one in turn departs in the night for an unknowable destination. Uneasiness, therefore, tormented souls, and men were seeking salvation. This aspiration was expressed most strikingly in the surname *soter*, "savior", which was given to so many ancient and newer divinities, to so many rulers also: the desire to be shielded from the threats of life and of death.

Against physical sufferings, people fervently invoked the
god of healing, Aesculapius. For ages he had had his sanc-
tuaries; the most famous were the shrines of Cos, in the
Aegean Sea, and of Epidaurus in Argolis. Crowds more
numerous than ever thronged to them. The reputation of its
medico-religious institute, where many students received
the formation that made physicians out of them, was one
of the chief causes for the prosperity of the island of Cos.

Those who could reassure man about the dangers beyond
the grave were helpful, merciful, and saving gods, too, and
even more than that. *Mors aurem vellens*, "Death pulls us
by the ear" (Virgil). They managed to do so by initiating
the believer into their mysteries. This form of religious
life then began a remarkable development in old or new
Greek shrines. The major trend, moreover, was toward
other mystery religions, because of the more dramatic and
emotional character of their ceremonies—so emotional that
accusations of charlatanism and debauchery began to cir-
culate against them. Dionysius, who was already present
in Eleusis, had his own mysteries, which spawned many
imitations. Neither the Greeks nor the Romans failed to
participate in other mystery religions associated with Oriental cults, such as the cults of Attis and Cybele in Asia
Minor, or those of Osiris and Isis in Egypt.

We know little about the details of these ceremonies,
about which the initiates had to keep silence. Certainly
the rites and formulas varied from one deity to the next.
Their object was to uproot from the believer's heart the
disastrous fear of so many miseries that overwhelmed him.
He attended the resurrection of a dead god and was thus
instructed in the secrets of death and rebirth. Perhaps the
mysteries of Eleusis stopped there, but the others led the
mystes, the initiate, further. After various purifications, he
became identified with the god and shared in his divine

nature. He confronted notions that the ancient Greek or Roman cults scarcely touched on: the concept of sin and the idea of purity, not just the physical sort that was attained by bathing and fasting, but moral purity. With promises of an incalculable reward, all this provided the initiate with a certain enrichment of his interior life, which until then had been left to fend for itself, but in the long run—alas!—it could not satisfy him.

The beginning of the Christian era was a great age of spiritual and religious journeys, a quest for truth, a search for the true God. One of these "God-seekers", the greatest among them, was Paul of Tarsus. He became the instrument chosen by the Lord to preach the universal religion in a common language, throughout an empire unified under the aegis of Rome.

2

Saul of Tarsus

The City

Tarsus on the river Tarsus, the Cydnus of antiquity, is today a somewhat sleepy city of sixty thousand inhabitants on the southeast coast of southern Anatolia, in modern-day Turkey.

In ancient times it was a city "not without renown", the origins of which went back to the old kingdom of the Hittites (1900–1200 B.C.). Although presently few monuments bear witness to its antiquity, its historical past is quite eventful. Over the course of the second millennium B.C. it was the capital of the Hittite state of Kizzuwatna, and in 698 B.C. it was captured by Sennacherib, king of Assyria. Alexander the Great stayed there in 333 B.C. after crossing through the narrow pass of the Gates of Cilicia. He nearly died of a fever that he contracted after bathing in the icy water of the Cydnus. Cicero, in his capacity as governor of Roman Cilicia, resided in Tarsus in 50 B.C., and Julius Caesar visited the city in 47 B.C. to meet there with representatives of the province.

Mark Antony lived there also, in 41 B.C., and rewarded the city for its resistance to Brutus and Cassius by exempting it from all taxes. During that same year he invited Cleopatra of Alexandria to Tarsus. She was the last representative of a Macedonian dynasty established on the Nile three hundred years previously by Ptolemy, a general of Alexander the Great. The queen's arrival was one of the most spectacular moments in the Greco-Roman history of Asia Minor, when, in her royal barge, with all the sails spread and banners flapping in the wind, to the sound of silver flutes, Cleopatra, the seventh by that name, traveled up the Cydnus—a scene described by Plutarch in his "Life of Mark Antony". She was even more seductive, people said, by her personal charm and the tone of her voice than by her genuine beauty. Shakespeare begins the account of this meeting in his *Antony and Cleopatra* with these memorable lines:

> The barge she sat in, like a burnished throne,
> Burn'd on the water: the poop was beaten gold,
> Purple the sails, and so perfumed that
> The winds were lovesick with them. The oars were
>   silver,
> Which to the tune of flutes kept stroke and made
> The water which they beat to follow faster....
>
> (Act 2, Scene 2)

Cleopatra was twenty-eight years old and Mark Antony fifty. Perhaps that was the occasion on which she had precious pearls dissolved into the drink that she offered him, during a sumptuous banquet in her honor.

In the motley crowd assembled on the riverbanks might we have found Saul's grandparents in that year 41 B.C.? It is quite possible. They belonged to the important Jewish community established in the city since the time of Antiochus III the Great (242?–187 B.C.). Paul himself said, "I am a Jew from Tarsus in Cilicia, a citizen of no mean city" (Acts 21:39).

The city of Tarsus, the old geographer Strabo also tells us, "very soon attained a great eminence in philosophy and other fields of knowledge, such that its love for science and the arts surpassed even the glory of Athens and Alexandria." The professors were almost all originally from Tarsus. Among the most famous were Antipater, the grammarian Artemidorus, Diodorus, and Dionysius, the tragedian. Demetrius visited Egypt and traveled to Great Britain to improve his knowledge of the world. Zeno the Stoic lived for a time in Tarsus and it was there, among the Eastern thinkers of the region, that he was introduced to philosophy.

Athenodorus, son of Sandon, became the counselor of the emperor Augustus and the tutor of young Claudius; he also helped Cicero to compose the *De Officiis*. Nestor the Academician was the tutor of Marcellus, the nephew of Augustus, and Nestor the Stoic was the tutor of Tiberius. That is why people used to say, "All teachers of thinking in Rome are from Tarsus." The poet Aratus (another Cilician) was so highly esteemed in Rome that Cicero himself translated his works into Latin, while Ovid declared, "Aratus will be with us forever, like the sun and the moon."

But all the scholars of Cilicia could not prevent the Cilicians from lapsing into the sorts of ungrammatical usage that are called "solecisms" from the name Soli (Pompeiopolis), a town situated at a distance of some thirty miles from Tarsus.

Not far from the gymnasium, the people venerated the sword of Apollo, which, miraculously, showed neither rust nor any deterioration. As a kind of charm, the Cilicians turned to Hermes *Eriounios* ("Helper", "good-luck bringer"), who appeared, purse in hand, on all their coins. In the case of sickness, the inhabitants, like everyone else in the Mediterranean basin, invoked Aesculapius, whose healing power was unequalled.

Every year in Anchiale, not far from Tarsus, the people celebrated the festival of Sacaea (*Sakaia* in Greek), a feast of

Babylonian origin that was handed down by the Persians; it was an occasion for debauchery and frenetic excesses. Apollonius of Tyana, who lived at the beginning of the Christian era, came to study rhetoric with the Phoenician Euthydamus. But the immorality in Tarsus was such that he begged his father for permission to leave the city and go to Aegae (modern Ayash on the coast), which was renowned for its reverence toward the gods and its learning.

A Young Jew Named Saul

The most famous personage from Tarsus is without a doubt the young Jew whom we know so well by the name of Paul, the apostle of the Gentiles.

He was born during the reign of Caesar Augustus between A.D. 6 and 10, was circumcised on the eighth day, and received the name of *Sh'aul*. This name means "desired" in Hebrew. His mother had prayed fervently for him, just as Hannah had prayed for Samuel (see 1 Sam 1:10–11). And like Hannah, she had consecrated him to the service of Yahweh (see Gal 1:15). Being a Roman citizen, he was registered in the archives of one of the Roman *tribus* ["tribes", a division of the state] in the capital, far, far away on the banks of the Tiber. Saul therefore went by two given names: *Sh'aul* among the Jews and *Paulos* among the Gentiles. His father was a citizen of Tarsus and a man of some importance in the city. Better yet, his status as a Roman citizen assured him of an eminent rank among his fellow citizens. His son, of course, enjoyed the same privileges when he reached the required age.

Saul was educated in the sect of the Pharisees, which was renowned for its piety and ardent patriotism (see Acts 22:3). Well before he was able to speak, they taught him to touch a metal box on the doorpost that contained the *mezūzāh*, a papyrus fragment inscribed with the Shema: "Hear, O Israel: The LORD is our God, the LORD is one." "*Sh'ma Yis'ra'eil, Adonai Eloheinu Adonai Echad*" (Deut 6:4).

Later, as he learned his first words, they taught him to face distant Jerusalem, hands uplifted to heaven, repeating the Shema or morning and evening prayer, as well as the text of a Scripture verse beginning and ending with the first and last letters of his Hebrew name.

Very early, too, the young boy, accompanied by his mother, went to the synagogue, where he took his place with her behind the *mechitzah*, the partition that separated them, along with the other women and children, from the men.

When they returned, his mother answered as well as she could the eager questions of her little boy, who gave evidence of a precocious maturity. In the evening, while she was sewing a garment for her son by the light of a somewhat smoky lamp, she would tell him the story of Abraham and Isaac, about Jacob, Joseph, and Moses; about Joshua, David, and Queen Esther; and finally about Daniel and about Judas Maccabeus, who had delivered the Jewish people from the tyrant Antiochus. She spoke to him also about the long-awaited Messiah who would deliver Israel and reestablish, once and for all, the glorious kingdom of King David.

When he had reached the age of five, his father took charge of his education. Children love to ask questions, and Saul must have been a walking question mark. Why do we eat *matzah* (unleavened bread) during Passover? For what reason does his father inspect by candlelight every nook and cranny of the house, which his mother has carefully swept to remove all traces of leaven? Then they would tell him about their deliverance from slavery as recorded in the Book of Exodus, chapter 12. In the month of December why do children bring palm branches to the synagogue? What is the reason then for lighting candles in the house and lanterns outside for eight days? Then they would explain to him how the wicked Antiochus had profaned the Temple and how Judas Maccabeus restored it to worship eleven years later. In the synagogue, why do the men furiously stamp their feet at the name of Haman and why do they bless the name of Esther? And what is the reason for distributing cakes and candles to the children as they leave the synagogue? And they would tell him the story of Queen Esther on the occasion of the feast of *Purim* (see Esther 9:29).

Why do children adorned with flowers bring garlands to the synagogue, which is surrounded by baskets of all sorts of fruit? Because it is the festival of the First Fruits (Pentecost), in the beautiful month of June, celebrated to thank God for the harvest (see Lev 23:9–11). Why are the neighbors all lined up outdoors, facing the east? They are waiting for the new moon, and the first to catch sight of it hurries to announce it at the synagogue (see Ps 81:3–4). We celebrate the occasion and everyone rejoices at the evening meal. And what's this? Even the Gentiles share in the festivity! On the occasion of the new year, the new moon is greeted with a grand salute of horns and trumpets.

Saul at School

Among the Jews, the school bore the picturesque name of "vineyard". They deemed that their children, like the grapevine, needed to be "cleaned" or pruned so as to produce fruit abundantly. But that did not mean draconian regimentation. To maintain order the teacher used (but only rarely) a leather strap, nothing else. At the age of six, accompanied by a slave, the pedagogue, who carefully watched over him and corrected him, even corporally, Saul began to attend the "vineyard". He was perhaps recalling this when he mentioned in his Letter to the Galatians "the law [which] was our custodian until Christ came" (Gal 3:24).

This sort of school was often in the open air, without desks or benches, without slates, pencils, or pens; without a blackboard, without maps, or diagrams. The pupils, seated on their heels at ground level, learned to read, write, and count by forming letters and numbers in the sand or on pieces of pottery, sometimes even on scraps of papyrus. The teacher recited a text out loud and the children repeated and repeated and repeated it until the lesson was firmly fixed in their memories. The shrill juvenile voices produced such a clamor that it gave rise to the proverbial expression "to cause an uproar like at school". The Jewish historian Flavius Josephus (Joseph ben Matthias) wrote in the first century A.D., "From the age of reason we learn the Law by heart, and it is, so to speak, anchored in our minds." The school was, of course, annexed to the synagogue, and it was also designated by the name of "House of the Book", since the books of the Law were the sole basis of all the instruction.

At home young Saul spoke the everyday language, that is, the Aramaic dialect of the region; at school they taught him the rudiments of ancient Hebrew and also *Koinē* Greek, the Greek that was commonly spoken in the Hellenic Roman Empire, the language of all the Jews of the Diaspora.

A small roll of papyrus containing excerpts from the Law hung at the right side of the door to his room—a constant reminder about the Law. Under his tunic he wore the prayer shawl made of fine fabric and edged at two corners with a tassel consisting of eight threads that was kissed during prayer at the synagogue, another reminder.

The Sabbath

Every Friday Saul's father stopped working early. As he entered his house, he touched his fingertips to the metal box, and kissed them, intoning the psalm verse "The LORD will keep your going out and your coming in from this time forth and for evermore" (Ps 121:8). Then he embraced his wife and children, who were waiting for him, dressed in their best tunics. He took Saul by the hand and murmured, "God make you as Ephraim and as Manasseh" (Gen 48:20). Then he turned to his daughter, placed his hand on her head, and blessed her in these words: "May Yahweh make you like Sarah and Rebekah" (see Gen 24:60). The house had previously been cleaned and put in order, and after taking a bath the father dressed as though for a feast.

At sunset the horn sounds at the synagogue, and at the same moment the silver trumpets resound in Jerusalem to announce to Jews throughout the world the beginning of *Shabbāth*, or the Sabbath. At home the door to the main room is closed. The family stands around the table while the two Sabbath candles, lit by the mother, project a yellowish light on the tablecloth, which is white as snow. The father purifies his fingers in a basin presented to him by one of the children and pronounces a blessing; he then fills a cup of wine mixed with water and gives each one a sip of it. While pronouncing a few words about Yahweh, the vine, and the Sabbath, he breaks the bread, salts it lightly, and distributes a piece to each person who is present. Everyone then sits down at table to enjoy the best meal of the week: some soup, fish, bread, fruits, and cakes, as well as wine from the vineyard. After the supper, they sing a prayer of thanksgiving. The ceremony ends with the reading of passages from Scripture in which the Sabbath is mentioned.

The following morning everyone goes to the synagogue, the house of Gathering, Assembly (*Beit ha-Knesset*), while looking neither to the left nor to the right. It is often a humble square or rectangular building, with a wooden or stone lintel that has been engraved with a vine, a bouquet of flowers, a seven-branched candelabra or a pot of manna. Sometimes the pediment also bears an inscription. The father covers his head, ties his phylacteries on his arm and forehead, and advances slowly toward the front, where the rulers of the synagogue are already gathered. Through the *mechitzah*, which separates them from the rest of the congregation, the women can catch sight of the great copper candelabra with seven branches, the *menorah*, as well as the sanctuary curtain, the *parochet*, richly decorated in purple, scarlet, blue, and gold. Behind the curtain is the Holy Ark of the Covenant that contains the scrolls of the sacred Scriptures. Above the Ark hangs a continuously burning lamp, the *ner tamid*. It symbolizes both the perpetual light burning in the Temple in Jerusalem and the unwavering presence of God. In the middle of the sanctuary is the raised platform, *bimah*, carrying the lectern for the reading of the Scriptures and the sermon.

The doors are closed. At the call of the "angel of the synagogue", the chazan (cantor) all rise and at the end of the first two prayers respond "Amen". Then comes the recitation of the Shema, made up of Deuteronomy 6:4–9; 11:14–21; Numbers 15:37–41. After a third prayer come the eighteen blessings, each one concluding with a vigorous Amen. The blessing of Numbers 15:37–41 concludes the liturgical part of the Sabbath.

A synagogue official then takes the scrolls of the Law and presents them to the lector, who reads (chants) the first lesson for the day in Hebrew, which is then translated verse by verse into the local language. In this way the whole

Torah, that is, the Pentateuch, is read by the end of a year. The second lesson, taken from the prophets, is also read and then translated three verses at a time. Once the reading is finished, the lector sits down and the congregation waits in silence for one of the persons present to speak to it. Any adult male is completely free to do so. If he is a rabbi, he delivers a sort of sermon, which in this case is called "the tail of the Torah", on the lesson of the day, during which comments made aloud by men in the assembly are not uncommon. Similarly, there could be a question period at the end of the sermon. Only on the occasion of a feast day is there singing, and a short blessing signals the end of the service.

On the Sabbath day no work is permitted and journeys (the Sabbath distance) cannot exceed two thousand cubits, or a little over half a mile. At the end of the day, when the sun sinks toward the west and the shadows over the city lengthen, the father or the mother gathers the family and pronounces a final blessing, and the Sabbath ends when the last gleam of light is gone from the horizon.

3

A Rabbinical Education

At the age of thirteen, Saul was admitted as a "son of the Law" or "son of the Commandment", *Bar Mitzvah* in Hebrew. After passing an examination on the contents of the sacred Scriptures, he was declared worthy to wear the phylacteries (*tefillim* in Hebrew), slips of parchment bearing Scripture verses and enclosed in two small calf-skin boxes attached to two long thongs. One of these boxes was fastened to his forehead, and the other was placed against the skin of his left arm, near the heart. The straps were wrapped seven times around his arm and three times around his hand and finally tied around the middle finger.

All this was to comply with Exodus 13:9–16, to bind the Commandments to one's hand and between one's eyes. The sermon for the occasion recalled the instruction that he should never enter the synagogue without his phylacteries, the symbol of his virility and of his total adherence to the Jewish religion. The day ended with a joyful meal. His mother, radiant and proud, could not help feeling a certain sadness because from then on, at the synagogue, her son would no longer come to sit beside her. Her young man, who already displayed a fiery temperament, with his breaking voice and just a hint of hair on his chin, stood in front of the congregation and proudly proclaimed, "Today I am a man."

In keeping with tradition, young Saul began an apprenticeship. As was customary, he too walked in the footsteps of his father, who was a tentmaker. He learned to weave *cilicium*, a rough material made from the long hair of the goats of Cilicia; the name has been preserved to this day in the French word *cilice*, "hair-shirt", a shirt or belt made of rough material and worn as a form of mortification.

Tents were made out of this goat's hair material and also out of animal skins; this is why Saint John Chrysostom (d. 417), in speaking about Saint Paul, describes him as a man who "sewed tents and cut out leather". Business was booming; the Roman armies in Asia Minor alone guaranteed full employment for tentmakers. Consequently this trade was very useful to Paul over the course of his missions to the Gentiles (see Acts 18:3; 20:34). On this subject he wrote to the Corinthians: "For we know that if the earthly tent we live in is destroyed, we have a building from God, a house not made with hands, eternal in the heavens" (2 Cor 5:1). Very early in his life Saul began to practice what he later preached: "If any one will not work, let him not eat" (2 Thess 3:10).

By the time he was fourteen years old, Saul had finished school, and his father, impressed by his precocious intelligence and maturity, had great plans for him. He wanted to send him to Jerusalem for higher studies conducted by the most famous and most learned rabbis of his time.

A trip to Jerusalem! O the thrill for the young lad! "I was glad when they said to me, 'Let us go to the house of the LORD!'" (Ps 122:1). After a farewell meal with the whole family and all their friends, during which he could not help feeling pangs of distress at the prospect of leaving his loved ones, Saul set out with a group of pilgrims for the radiant city.

The journey was not without danger, for it was not uncommon to encounter highway bandits, pillagers, and thieves. Every evening, before the end of the daylight, Saul prepared his main meal. When night fell he stretched out on his mat and pensively watched the earth go to sleep and saw the bronze-colored diamonds of the stars scintillating in the velour of the night sky; it seemed that by simply extending his arm he could gather a handful of them. But very quickly, under the celestial vault that swung around him, he slept a deep, dreamless sleep of an adolescent.

Entering the Syrian Gates (or Bailan Pass), the caravan plunged into the Amanus mountains, where at night it had to contend with wolves and hyenas and sometimes, too, in the middle of the day, with hungry tigers.

After passing through Antioch of Syria, the third largest city of the world after Rome and Alexandria, Saul and his companions took the road to Damascus. Traveling due south toward the hills of Bashan, Saul, for the first time in his life, walked on the soil of his ancestors. From there he spied the snow-capped cone of Mount Hermon and the chain of mountains in Lebanon, covered with cedars and famous throughout the Eastern world. At that time the land was governed in the name of the emperor, Tiberius, by the procurator Annius Rufus.

The road followed the valley of the impetuous Jordan River to the Sea of Galilee or of Tiberias, which is 13 miles long, 7.5 miles wide, and situated 690 feet below sea level. Overlooking the lake on its southwestern shore is the city of Tiberias, a new Roman city in the midst of Jewish territory, founded at the beginning of the Christian era by Herod Antipas. From there one can see Mount Tabor, where Barak and Deborah triumphed over Sisera and his chariots of war. Further on, the travelers discovered the Plain of Esdraelon, famous for the many battles that were waged there, as well as Mount Gilboa, where King Saul killed himself, mistakenly convinced that he had lost the fight.

As a precaution, the main road followed the eastern shore of the lake, because Jewish pilgrims were often attacked by the Samaritans, schismatic Jews who worshipped on Mount Gerizim, in Shechem. There Jacob and his sons had stopped en route to Hebron to pay a visit to Isaac. Located there too were Jacob's well and Joseph's tomb. Soon they entered the narrow valley of Yabbok at Gilead, where Jacob had wrestled the whole night with the Angel of the Lord and dislocated his thigh (see Gen 32:25–30). From the other side of the lake they discerned through the fog the village of Bethel. At that place the same Jacob saw in a dream angels ascending and descending "a ladder set up on the earth, and the top of it reached to heaven" (Gen 28:12).

Saul bathed in the cold water of the Jordan, at the place where Joshua had forded the river more than a thousand years previously (see Josh 3:1), and soon reached Jericho in the land of the tribe of Benjamin, the tribe of his ancestors. The famous city of Jericho, whose fortified walls crumbled tumultuously at the sound of the trumpets and the ram's horn! Here was Gilgal, the place where the people came looking for David to bring him in triumph to Jerusalem (see 2 Sam 19:15); Ramah, where Samuel lived and taught (see 1 Sam 7:17); Mizpah, the place where Saul was proclaimed king (see 1 Sam 10:17). Farther on Saul caught sight of the dazzlingly white Rock of Rimmon; in that place six hundred men of his tribe resisted the enemy for four months (see Judg 20:47). Upon leaving the valley of Jericho, Saul and his companions took a deep gorge through the hills of Judaea. It is called "The Bloody Path" because in that place pilgrims were often plundered and sometimes assassinated.

After Bethany and the slope of the Mount of Olives, Saul could not believe his eyes. He gasped at the sight. Before him loomed Mount Moriah. That was where Abraham had come to sacrifice Isaac, his only son (see Gen 22:2). It was also the site of the magnificent Temple of Solomon, destroyed in 568 B.C. by the Babylonians and rebuilt during the reign of Herod the Great. It was a dazzling edifice made of white marble, with a perimeter of almost a mile. And beyond it, strategically situated, was Mount Sion, the city of the great King David.

The rustling of the palm branches! The singing of psalms! The Songs of Ascents repeated in chorus by the pilgrims. And the descent from the Mount of Olives by the plunging, winding road of the Kidron Valley, down to the bridge where the weary traveler can peer down at the watercourse so dearly beloved by David. "There is a river whose streams make glad the city of God, the holy habitation of the Most High" (Ps 46:4).

The pilgrims have arrived at their destination. They exclaim to one another, "Our feet have been standing within your gates, O Jerusalem!" (Ps 122:2). They clamber up the precipitous road until they reach the stairs that lead to the first marble courtyard, where the dove vendors offer their wares in wicker cages and where the sheepfold for the sacrificial lambs is located. The moneychangers are there, too, seated behind long tables loaded with coins from all the major Greek cities of the Roman Empire.

The din is deafening, and so Saul and his companions hurry toward the court of the Gentiles. They reach the *Soreg*, a stone wall perforated with narrow doors and decorated with little columns topped with tablets bearing the notice in Greek and Latin:

No Gentile can enter by this door
Or penetrate into the enclosure of this sanctuary.
Any transgressor is solely responsible
For the ensuing punishment of death.

This wall, therefore, is the barrier that separates the Gentiles and the Jews: "For he [Christ] is our peace, who has made us both one [people], and has broken down the dividing wall of hostility" (Eph 2:14).

After marveling at the magnificent Beautiful Gate, Saul finds himself in the Courtyard of Women under the open sky. From there he can identify the lodgings of the priests and Levites as well as the storehouses of food, oil, salt, wine, and other items necessary for worship. He notices also, to the right, the Treasury building, the most secure place in the whole Jewish world, where money and precious objects are kept. The wealth stored up inside its walls was prodigious because at the same time the Temple tax collected from the entire Jewish Diaspora was deposited there.

At the entrance to the courtyard stood the collection boxes, with horn-shaped openings, and Saul made his contribution, just like the poor widow who put in two small coins (see Lk 21:2).

Crossing the courtyard, Saul climbed the steps leading to the Gate of Nicanor, made of Corinthian bronze, and pressed on into the Court of Israelites, which was reserved for men. From there he could see the great altar built with white uncut stones, billowing smoke from the perpetual fire of the sacrifices. He remembered his mother telling him that not even two hundred years before Antiochus Epiphanes, king of Syria, had conquered Jerusalem and profaned the Temple by sacrificing swine on that altar and by erecting a statue of Zeus in the courtyard. What a scandal that was! A little farther on, he noticed priests slaughtering the lambs and collecting their blood in gold and silver basins. Another much larger basin, set upon twelve bronze lions, was so enormous that it was called "the sea": that was where the priests purified themselves after the sacrifices.

He advanced farther and, somewhat higher, Saul set foot on a third terrace adorned with immense blocks of stone covered with golden plaques, from which graceful columns soared up, supporting a gilded roof topped with a crown made of iron spearheads, flashing beneath the fiery sky of Judaea. Saul turned to face the Holy of Holies, the innermost sanctuary of the Temple, with its golden door hidden behind a thick curtain woven of blue, scarlet, purple, and white. All were forbidden to enter by that door except the high priest, who crossed the threshold only once a year.

To the northeast, near the Sheep Gate, the somber Tower of Antony loomed ominously; it was occupied by a garrison of Roman soldiers who kept an eye on the crowd, ready to quell disorderly conduct or put down any attempt at rebellion. Herod had built that tower to make it his palace and had named it in honor of Mark Antony.

The Jewish Passover

On the day before the full moon, Saul bought his lamb and brought it to the Temple so that it could be examined minutely by the priest, for the male animal had to be less than a year old and without blemish. He patiently waited in the Priests' Courtyard until the sun had set. The silver trumpets sounded, the gates opened slowly, and the crowd squeezed inside. The knives plunged into the lambs' necks; their blood was collected at the foot of the altar and disposed of in a great stream of water brought from the hills of Hebron by an aqueduct built by the great king Solomon.

Meanwhile, in the Women's Courtyard, the choir of Levites sang psalms, and at each pause the crowd responded enthusiastically Alleluia. The lambs were skinned rapidly, hung on gilded hooks, and cut into pieces. The priest kept one part for the altar and another for himself, while Saul took the rest, which would then be grilled at the campsite for the paschal meal. He shared it with his friends while eating the unleavened bread, in Hebrew *matzah*, and bitter herbs in memory of the evil days of slavery in Egypt and the deliverance of the people of Israel.

Rabbinical Formation

At that time in Jerusalem there were two rabbinical schools, one founded by Shammai and the other by Hillel. Both belonged to the sect of the Pharisees and taught the Law of Moses, but Shammai preached a broad interpretation of the Law while Hillel tended to follow the strict tradition. The disputes between the two schools eventually became so virulent that they gave rise to the Jewish saying "Even Elijah the Tishbite could not reconcile the disciples of Shammai and Hillel."

Saul enrolled in the school founded by Hillel (30 B.C.– A.D. 10) and directed in his day by Gamaliel (nicknamed "The Splendor of the Law"), one of the seven who merited the title "Rabban", which was given to the most illustrious doctors of the Law, whose counsel was golden. Gamaliel had won the esteem of his people and even that of the emperor Tiberius.

The teacher, on a sort of platform, was surrounded by his disciples, who sat on the ground, "powdered with dust, at the feet of the sages". He would choose a passage from the Torah and explain all that the rabbis had said about it in the past, commenting on the merits of their opinions. The students then debated the question with the teacher and among themselves. Day after day, month after month, it was explanations, questions and answers, objections, clarifications, ad infinitum, and since they were all modeled on the same format, occasionally it must have caused profound weariness. In that way they studied the Torah (the Pentateuch) but also the Prophets (*Nevi'im*) and the Writings (*Kethuvim*).

"I advanced in Judaism beyond many of my own age among my people, so extremely zealous was I for the traditions of my fathers" (Gal 1:14). Therefore Saul made great progress in his study of the Law and the traditions. He became a very intense and even fanatical Pharisee, as well as an ardent patriot. His knowledge of the Scriptures was such that, when he cited it, it was most often from memory, as certain experts have remarked. His citations come from 141 chapters of the Pentateuch and more than two hundred verses of thirty-three psalms and from nineteen chapters of Isaiah. Almost all of them are taken from the Greek Septuagint. According to the legend, this version was composed by seventy-two doctors of the Law in seventy-two days (or, in round numbers, seventy, *septuaginta*) at the command of Ptolemy II Philadelphus, in Alexandria in Egypt.

"Accursed be the one who eats pork, and accursed be the one who teaches the wisdom of the Greeks", says the Jewish proverb. But Gamaliel had defied that prejudice. He regularly visited a Greek philosopher and called him his friend and colleague. His son, Simeon, mentions that "my father's school had more than a thousand students: half of them studied the Jewish law and the other half the *sophia* [wisdom] of the Greeks."

We can safely assume that Saul had pretty close contacts with representatives of the school of Greek wisdom. He wields the Greek language not like someone who has learned it laboriously, late in life, but like a cultivated man who absorbed it from his earliest youth. He cites Epimenides, Aratus, Menander, and uses more than thirty Greek figures of speech. Probably, he had listened to recitations from Thucydides as well as from Pindar, Euripides,

and Aristophanes. The same goes for the teaching of the
Stoics. Did he perhaps read Seneca, who was a contemporary? Just as Moses was an expert in the wisdom of
the Egyptians, so too Saul drew upon the Greek wisdom
handed down by the Hellenic culture.

At the conclusion of his rabbinical formation and after
a final examination, Saul was allowed to be seated among
the rabbis. They presented to him a writing tablet covered
by a thin film of wax, signifying his duty to teach; then
he received a key that symbolically opened the treasures
of knowledge and wisdom. After hands were imposed on
him—a gesture that signifies the transmission of authority
or an office—he received teaching faculties and the right
to be called by the title rabbi, or teacher.

Once his studies were completed, Paul no doubt returned
to Tarsus, where he began to teach the Law and the Prophets: the enormous number of rules and regulations, 613 of
them in the Torah alone, had become a heavy burden for
every orthodox Jew. Saul did not forget this later, after his
conversion, when he turned to the Gentiles and refused to
impose that now useless burden on them. He also began, no
doubt with his father, to practice his trade as a *skēnopoiòs*,
or "tentmaker", so as to earn his living.

Several years later, perhaps on the occasion of a pilgrimage, he returned to Jerusalem, where the college of the
doctors of the Law convinced him to stay. He visited the
synagogue of the Cilicians and, around A.D. 35 or 36, to
his great indignation, he had to deal with the sect of that
Joshua whom his disciples proclaimed to be the Lord's
Anointed, *Khrestos* in Greek.

That encounter and its consequences would completely
upset his life.

4

Metanoia, or the Conversion of Saul

John the Baptist had preached repentance in the desert and baptized Jesus in the Jordan and was then beheaded in the prison of Machaerus at the orders of Herod Antipas.

The Lord's Anointed, the Christ, had come to perform miracles and to preach the Word of God; he had died ignominiously on the Cross but was risen from the dead; he had commanded his apostles to propagate the New Way and had then ascended into heaven.

Peter had preached on the day of Pentecost and converted three thousand people. Joseph of Cyprus, a Levite or assistant to the Temple priests, sold his parcel of land and placed the proceeds at the feet of the apostles. They nicknamed him Barnabas, or the "Son of Consolation". Ananias and Sapphira sold their property, too, but lied about its value and died a horrible death.

The apostles were thrown in prison and the Sanhedrin was preparing to execute them when Gamaliel intervened with the council to have them spared (see Acts 5:34–39). The disciples increased in number and elected seven "deacons", from *diakonos*, "servant", in Greek, to assist the apostles in caring for the poor and in administering the material goods of what they were already starting to call the *ekklesia* [church].

Stephen, filled with the Holy Spirit, was one of those deacons, but at the same time he preached the good news in the synagogues; there was a great number of them in those days in Jerusalem because Jews from all over the Diaspora were staying there. One could attend the synagogue of the Libertini, of the Jews sold into slavery who later, at the order of the Roman emperor, had been freed. Or another one where the Jews from Alexandria gathered; or yet another for the people of Cyrene, in present-day Libya. There was one for the Jews from the Roman province of Asia, which had Ephesus as its capital. And Paul, as was only right, attended the synagogue of Cilicia.

The Jewish zealots debated furiously with Stephen without ever having the last word, which increased even more their hatred toward him. Was Paul one of them?

Stephen was arrested and brought before the Sanhedrin, an assembly made up of seventy-one members. His enemies produced false witnesses: "This man never ceases to speak words against this holy place and the law" (Acts 6:13). All those who sat in the Sanhedrin had their eyes fixed on him, and they "saw that his face was like the face of an angel" (6:15). The high priest asked him: "Is this so?" (7:1). Stephen answered him with a long and very beautiful speech, without sparing his accusers, whom he characterized as "stiff-necked...uncircumcised in heart and ears" (7:51). At these words "they were enraged, and they ground their teeth against him" (7:54). Guilty or not guilty? They condemned him to death, dragged him outside the city, and stoned him. Meanwhile Stephen prayed, "'Lord Jesus, receive my spirit.' And he knelt down and cried with a loud voice, 'Lord, do not hold this sin against them.' And when he had said this, he fell asleep" (7:59–60).

Paul was part of the group and consented to this murder. His status as a rabbi did not prevent him from participating actively in it, but he was content to watch over the murderers' garments. As for Stephen, whose name in Greek means "crown", he was the first in the history of the Church to receive the crown of martyrdom.

Just as a wild boar in a vegetable garden or a flower bed destroys everything in its path, so too Paul "laid waste the church, and entering house after house, he dragged off men and women and committed them to prison" (Acts 8:3; see 22:4). The persecution of the Christians, however, had beneficial effects. Christ had commanded his disciples to preach the good news to all nations, but they had remained in Jerusalem. The persecution dispersed them and, like sparks carried by storm winds, they spread the fire of the gospel everywhere.

After his success in the Jewish capital, Saul looked for other territories to conquer. "Still breathing threats and murder against the disciples of the Lord" (Acts 9:1), Saul went to the high priest and asked him for letters of introduction to the synagogues of Damascus, a city situated some 150 miles from Jerusalem, as well as warrants for the arrest of Christians so that he might bring them to Jerusalem to be condemned.

Saul knew that road very well. It is the one that led him to Tarsus, to his parents' house. He left the city by the Gate of Damascus, climbed the hill where, on the left, the tombs of the Judges were located, and continued as far as Ramah in the territory of the tribe of Benjamin, to which he belonged (see 1 Kings 15:17). Further on he could discern, through the fog, Gibeah (see 1 Sam 10:26), the birthplace of King Saul, from which Jonathan set out to disperse the Philistines. On his right he passed Gibeon (see Josh 10:12). There the sun stopped to allow Joshua to win the battle and there also the Tabernacle [containing the Ark of the Covenant] had been set up for many years during the reigns of Saul and David.

At Shiloh Saul no doubt recalled Eli and the young Samuel (1 Sam 1:3), and from there he could survey the heights of Jezreel, where Saul met his death. Beyond the hills of Ephraim he descended into the valleys of Ebal and Gerizim as far as Jacob's well. That is where Jesus offered the water of eternal life to the sinful woman of Samaria.

Farther to the east lies the village of Dothan, where Joseph was sold into slavery by his brothers (see Gen 37:28). Saul then went into Galilee and crossed the Jordan at the Bridge of Jacob's Daughters. A few miles north of the lake, he caught sight of the imposing summit of Mount Hermon high in the blue sky. And his journey continued, through the valley of the Jordan, which he soon left to head for Syria through a desert landscape.

Damascus! "The Eye of the Desert", the "Pearl of the Orient", the oldest continually inhabited city in the world. Eliezer, the faithful servant of Abraham, was originally from Damascus. David stationed at that city a garrison that subsequently opposed Solomon's plans. Naaman of Damascus was cured by Elisha (see 2 Kings 5). The plums of Damascus were famous, along with its damask linen and its damascened swords.

Saul was approaching the city when—what is happening? We can read the account of this event in the statement that Paul made in the presence of Herod Agrippa.

At midday, O king, I saw on the way a light from heaven, brighter than the sun, shining round me and those who journeyed with me. And when we had all fallen to the ground, I heard a voice saying to me in the Hebrew language, "Saul, Saul, why do you persecute me? It hurts you to kick against the goad." And I said, "Who are you,

Lord?" And the Lord said, "I am Jesus whom you are persecuting." (Acts 26:13–15)

Instantly Paul's soul and mind were completely transformed. He accepted the heavenly vision and gave himself totally to Christ: "Lord, what do you want me to do?" The revelation of Christ brought about a complete revolution in Paul's life. The anti-Christian Jew was replaced by the gospel Christian.

At Damascus there is a tradition that identifies the village of Kawbab, situated near the city, as the place of Saint Paul's conversion. Every year on January 25 the Christians come in procession, reading the account from the Acts of the Apostles. Every year also on the same date the Catholic Church commemorates that event, which was of capital importance in her history.

Just as an earthquake can change the course of a river or a stream, so too the apparition of the Risen Savior completely changed the life of Paul of Tarsus. Saul the Pharisee became Paul the Nazarene. The great persecutor of the Christians became the apostle of Christ. The Risen Lord "appeared also to me", just as he did to the other apostles; therefore Paul is in no way inferior to them (1 Cor 15:8; see 9:1). Based on his personal experience he could testify to the resurrection of Christ and to his glorious and everlasting life.

Paul had "kicked against the goads", a well-known proverb in antiquity used by Aeschylus, Euripides, and Terence, among others. He could not resist the heavenly vision, however (see Acts 26:19). "Lord, what do you want me to do?" The Lord told him, "Rise and enter the city, and you will be told what you are to do" (Acts 9:6). Paul stood up and although his eyes were open he saw nothing: "So they led him by the hand and brought him into

Damascus. And for three days he was without sight, and
neither ate nor drank" (9:8–9).

He was welcomed into the house of a certain Judas on
Straight Street. Almost 1.25 miles long, it connected the
eastern gate to the one in the west; the street was one
hundred feet wide and was divided into three avenues by
elegant Corinthian colonnades.

The Lord spoke to a disciple in Damascus by the name
of Ananias and told him to meet with Paul. But Ananias
replied, "Lord, I have heard from many about this man,
how much evil he has done to your saints at Jerusalem;
and here he has the authority from the chief priests to bind
all who call upon your name." But the Lord said to him,
"Go, for he is a chosen instrument of mine to carry my
name before the Gentiles and kings and the sons of Israel;
for I will show him how much he must suffer for the sake
of my name" (Acts 9:13–16).

Ananias obeyed, entered the house, laid his hands on Saul
and said to him: "'Brother Saul, the Lord Jesus who appeared
to you on the road by which you came, has sent me that you
may regain your sight and be filled with the Holy Spirit.'
And immediately something like scales fell from his eyes and
he regained his sight. Then he rose and was baptized, and
took food and was strengthened" (Acts 9:17–19).

Paul spent several days with the disciples in Damascus
and began without delay to preach in the synagogues, proclaiming that Jesus is the Son of God. "All who heard him
were amazed, and said, 'Is not this the man who made
havoc in Jerusalem of those who called on this name? And
he has come here for this purpose, to bring them bound
before the chief priests'" (Acts 9:21).

After a journey to Arabia (see Gal 1:17–18), Paul
returned to Damascus; his powers of persuasion continued
to increase. He confounded the Jews of the city, proving

that Jesus was the Lord's Anointed. After a while the Jews had had enough, and they planned to kill him. For this purpose they kept watch at the city gates day and night.

Paul was aware of their plot. The ethnarch (governor) appointed by Aretas IV, king of Petra, "guarded the city of Damascus in order to seize me, but I was let down in a basket through a window in the wall, and escaped his hands" (2 Cor 11:32–33).

This Aretas was the father-in-law of Herod Antipas; the latter repudiated his wife in A.D. 29 and seduced the wife of his brother Philip, for which he was severely reprimanded by John the Baptist. For reasons that are unknown the emperor Tiberius ordered Vitellius, the proconsul, to seize Aretas, dead or alive. News of the death of Tiberius reached Vitellius in Jerusalem in April of A.D. 37, and so the order was not carried out. Gaius Caligula, the new emperor, was a friend of Aretas and offered him Damascus during an adjustment of boundaries.

Paul set out for Jerusalem, "to visit Cephas" (Gal 1:18). The Greek expression *historêsai* actually means "to question, to confer with". Upon his arrival he tried to join the disciples, but they all feared him and did not believe that he had become one of them. Then Joseph, the Levite from Cyprus who was nicknamed Barnabas,

> took him, and brought him to the apostles, and declared to them how on the road he had seen the Lord, who spoke to him, and how at Damascus he had preached boldly in the name of Jesus. So he went in and out among them at Jerusalem, preaching boldly in the name of the Lord. And he spoke and disputed against the Hellenists [i.e., Greek-speaking Jews]; but they were seeking to kill him. And when the brethren knew it, they brought him down to Caesarea [Stratonis on the coast], and sent him off to Tarsus. (Acts 9:27–31)

No doubt Paul took the land route, preaching along the way, of course, because later he tells Agrippa that he had proclaimed the good news all along the coast of Judaea and then to the Gentiles. And he adds, "Then I went into the regions of Syria and Cilicia." He remained there for fourteen years (Gal 1:21; see 2:1). What did he do during that long period of time? He founded churches and returned to them repeatedly to strengthen them in the faith (see Acts 15:41). And the churches of Judaea gave thanks to the Lord. "They...heard it said, 'He who once persecuted us is now preaching the faith he once tried to destroy.' And they glorified God because of me" (Gal 1:23–24).

Many citizens of Tarsus converted, and when they became Christians they got rid of their idols, a large number of which have been discovered by archaeologists. In A.D. 110, Dio Chrysostom praised the women of Tarsus for their modesty. They were completely veiled when they went walking in the street. In 160 Abgarbarman added the cross to the design stamped on coins and prohibited the practice of castration in honor of the goddess Cybele. Diodorus of Antioch became bishop of Tarsus in 378 and taught Theodore of Mopsuestia and John Chrysostom, the "golden-tongued" preacher.

Paul in Antioch of Syria

Fifteen miles from the mouth of the Orontes River, Seleucus Nicator (the Conqueror) founded a city around the year 300 B.C., which he combined with the small market town Antigonia and named it after his father, Antiochus. Over the course of his life he built sixteen Antiochs, nine Seleucias to perpetuate his own name, six Laodiceas in honor of his mother, and one city named Apamea for his wife. Seleucus Epiphanes enlarged the city and encircled it with a girdle of solid earthworks. In 65 B.C. Pompey captured it but granted it a certain degree of autonomy. Julius Caesar built a basilica known by the name of Caesarium. Augustus added a suburb to the city and circus grounds that reportedly could accommodate almost forty thousand people. Tiberius repaired the crumbling walls, and Gaius Caligula had baths constructed as well as an aqueduct. Herod the Great saw to it that the main road running east to west was paved for 2.5 miles with blocks of white marble and bordered on either side with a magnificent colonnade, under which one could go for a walk in any weather. Titus, the emperor, adorned the western gate with a colossal gilded cherub originally from the Temple of Jerusalem.

Antioch, with its approximately 350,000 inhabitants, was the third most important city of the empire and was often called the second Rome. As the capital of Syria it was equipped with a strong Roman garrison. The city was renowned for its high level of culture, but that did not keep it from being prey to a number of charlatans, notably one Debborius who sold amulets as protection against earthquakes. The fortune-tellers found their best clients among the leisured class. To appease the wrath of the gods during an epidemic, Leius received an order to sculpt the face of Charon on the southern side of the enormous peak of Mount Silpius. Charon is the ferryman in Greek mythology who, for an obol [a coin worth a quarter of a drachma], transported the shades of the departed into Hades. This monument was called the Charonium, and one can get some idea of it, thanks to the bronze coins that were struck with his effigy.

Antioch was the birthplace and residence of the poet Archias, in whose defense Cicero composed his classic *Defense of Poetry*. Libanius (314–393), the brilliant professor, Sophist, and counselor of Julian the Apostate, praises his

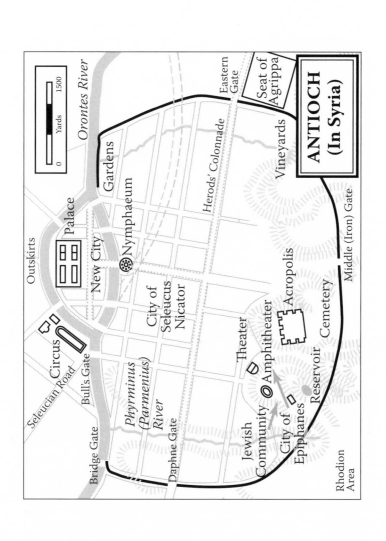

ANTIOCH
(In Syria)

Orontes River

0   Yards   1500

Outskirts

Seleucian Road

Circus

Bull's Gate

Bridge Gate

Palace

New City

Gardens

Nymphaeum

City of
Seleucus
Nicator

Phyrminus
(Parmenius)
River

Daphne Gate

Herods' Colonnade

Eastern
Gate

Seat of
Agrippa

Vineyards

Theater

Amphitheater

Jewish
Community

City of
Epiphanes

Acropolis

Reservoir

Cemetery

Middle (Iron) Gate

Rhodion
Area

native city for the abundance and excellence of its water. "Every citizen has water in his house. The water is so clear that the bucket seems to be empty and so pleasing to the taste that it incites one to drink." The streets of Antioch were illuminated at night—something unique among the cities of antiquity—by oil lamps, so well that (as Libanius boasted) there was no difference between day and night.

Some forty stadia, which is to say almost 4.5 miles from Antioch, in a wood, Daphne, the daughter of a mythological river god, refused Apollo's advances and was transformed into a laurel tree. At that place Seleucus built a famous temple surrounded by a magnificent park through which several streams ran, making the atmosphere pleasantly cool. The statue of Apollo by Bryaxis was, according to Ammianus Marcellinus, at least equal in beauty to that of the Olympian Jupiter. Temples dedicated to Artemis and Isis were likewise erected. Antiochus Epiphanes built a stadium there, the revenues from which were used to organize the annual games.

That park in honor of Daphne was the site of a permanent festival of vice, a celebration resounding with the bellowing of drums and cavernous cymbals that combined with the howling chorus of Corybants, so that the expression "Morals of Daphne" had become a proverb. "Even the peasant, soldier or philosopher avoided the temptations of that sensual paradise, where pleasure assumed the character of religion" (Gibbon). Avidius Cassius, the intrepid general of Marcus Aurelius, forbade his soldiers, under penalty of imprisonment, to frequent the place. All of the commerce, the architecture, the literature, the philosophy—in a word, all the culture of Antioch—could not prevent the population from falling into the most degrading sensuality. Seneca speaks about Rome as a cesspool of iniquity, but Juvenal compared the Eternal City to a nauseating sewer made even worse by the torrent of vice poured into the Tiber by the Syrian Orontes.

Following the stoning of Stephen, the new believers in Jesus Christ dispersed into Phoenicia, Cyprus, and even as far as North Africa. Others headed for Antioch, preaching the Risen Christ to the Hellenized Jews and even to the Gentiles. "And the hand of the Lord was with them, and a great number that believed turned to the Lord" (Acts 11:21).

News of these conversions reached the ears of the apostles in Jerusalem. Anxious to know more about it, they assigned Barnabas to go to Antioch and report on the situation. He found the grace of God at work and rejoiced; he exhorted the new converts to remain steadfastly faithful to the Lord.

A simple report was not sufficient; they had to find a man capable of directing the new community. Barnabas knew where to find him. He set out immediately for Tarsus, a journey of about 155 miles, to look for Paul in his native city. After finding him he brought him back to Antioch, probably in the year 43. For a whole year they worked together in the Lord's vineyard, and a considerable crowd joined the new Church.

That may have taken place on Singon Street, near the Pantheon and the Forum, one of the most popular quarters in the southeast part of the city, which was called Epiphania. In that Syrian Sodom the crucified Christ was proclaimed. And what was the result? "In Antioch the disciples were for the first time called Christians" (Acts 11:26).

When Agabus predicted a famine in Palestine, the Christians of Antioch endeavored to help their brethren in Judaea, each according to his means, and sent the funds to the deacons through the agency of Barnabas and Paul. This occurred probably in the year 45, after the apostle James the Great was put to death and Peter was imprisoned by Herod Agrippa.

Suetonius mentions the exorbitant prices resulting from the famine during the reign of the emperor Claudius, while Tacitus and Dio Cassius speak of two famines in Rome. Flavius Josephus explains that the famine raged at the time of Cuspius Fadus and Liberius Alexander (A.D. 44–48), both of whom were prefects of Rome under Claudius. He adds that the queen of Syria, Helen of Adiabene, a Jewish proselyte, traveled to Jerusalem in the year 48 and had grain imported from Alexandria and figs from Cyprus to feed the poor of the country.

At that time, in the Church of Antioch, there were prophets and teachers such as Barnabas; Symeon, who was called Niger; Lucius of Cyrene; Manaen, a childhood friend of Herod Antipas the Tetrarch; and Paul (see Acts 13:1). Now one day "while they were worshipping the Lord and fasting, the Holy Spirit said, 'Set apart for me Barnabas and Saul for the work to which I have called them.' Then after fasting and praying they laid their hands on them and sent them off" (13:2–3).

The Church of Antioch had the great honor of being the first to send missionaries, Paul and Barnabas, to the Gentiles. Of course there were still many pagans to convert in Antioch; nevertheless the Holy Spirit commanded them to leave the city and go "make disciples of all nations" (Mt 28:19).

Antioch was not weakened by the loss of those zealous preachers. It remained, until the Arab invasions, a firm bastion of Christianity in the Near East. Some sixty years later, Ignatius, one of its most famous bishops, was arrested at the command of the emperor Trajan and was brought to Rome and thrown to the lions. Subsequently Antioch became the center of a school of Christian theology, and ten synods were convened there between 252 and 380. John Chrysostom was born there in 347, and he tells us that the city then numbered more than two hundred thousand inhabitants, half of them Christians. When Julian the Apostate came to stay in the city to celebrate a pagan festival, the only sacrifice to the Apollo in the park of Daphne was his own, "except for a goose offered by the priest, the solitary inhabitant of that ruined temple", as the ineffable Gibbon informs us. In 362 lightning destroyed the temple and the image of Apollo. Julian immediately blamed the Christians of Antioch and, convinced of their guilt, ordered reprisals. He had the leading church of the city closed, and the precious ornaments that had been given to it by the emperors Constantine and Constans were pillaged. There were other depredations in response to that fire, but the documents that we still have today give us very few details in this regard.

The emperor Julian left Antioch on March 5, 363, to go strike at the heart of the enemy empire of Persia. He did not return from the campaign but died in battle, struck by a cavalryman's lance, on June 26 of that same year. He had not completed his thirty-second year and had been emperor for a year and eight months. John Chrysostom was sixteen years old then, and the future Saint Augustine, nine.

5

The First Missionary Journey

Journey to Cyprus

Three men in long robes, with a bag over the shoulders and a staff in hand, their faces protected from the sun, journeyed on the dusty road that led to Seleucia Pieiria ("Sumptuous"). They had left Antioch at cock's crow and headed for the great port of Syria built by Seleucus Nicator at the mouth of the Orontes, where his tomb was located. One can still see today, several feet underwater, the stones of the great pier. Some of them are almost 6.5 feet long by 6.5 feet wide, and 5 feet thick, joined together by impressive grappling irons.

From that port our travelers—Paul, Barnabas, and their assistant John Mark—would set sail the following day for the island of Cyprus, thus beginning their first missionary journey.

From the word "Cyprus", in Greek *Kupros*, we have received the terms "cypress" and "copper". Caesar Augustus offered to lease out the island's copper mines to Herod the Great, and consequently a large number of Jews were sent to Cyprus. They became so numerous that in the year 117, under Armenius, they rebelled and massacred a large number of the inhabitants. The emperor Hadrian harshly put down the revolt and forbade all Jewish presence on the island under pain of death, even in case of shipwreck.

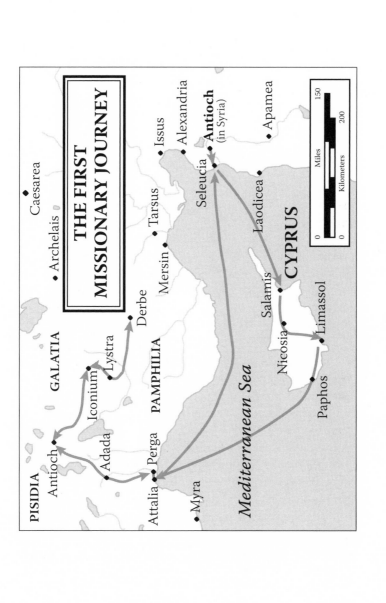

THE FIRST
MISSIONARY JOURNEY

Since Teucer had not avenged the death of Ajax, his father, Telaemon, king of Salamis, banished him from the city. Teucer took refuge at the eastern extremity of the island and founded there another city, likewise named Salamis. There he introduced human sacrifices in honor of Zeus, which were not prohibited until the time of Hadrian, in the second century of the Christian era.

A rapid crossing, with favorable winds, from sunrise to sunset, covered the 69 miles separating Seleucia from Salamis and brought our travelers to their destination.

Without delay they set about their work of speaking to the Jews in the synagogues of the city. They visited Citium, the Chittim of the Old Testament, the birthplace of Zeno, the Stoic philosopher, and the burial place of Cimon, the son of Miltiades. Located nearby was the market town of Amathus, famous for its copper mines. They continued their journey as far as Paphos, situated not far from the shrine of Astarte, Aphrodite, and Venus, around a hundred miles distant from Salamis.

Hesiod and Homer say that here a drop of fecund blood fell from the sky, from Uranus, into the Cyprian Sea, which was greatly agitated, and out of the pearly white froth of the waves Aphrodite was born. One of the largest temples dedicated to that goddess had been built here; it comprised more than a hundred altars. Her sacred image was a phallus of polished white marble, the symbol of generation. Mothers brought their daughters to prostitute themselves there, and part of the proceeds was reserved for them to serve as a dowry.

Noctuvigilia. That is what Plautus calls the festivals held in honor of Venus. Homer informs us that they lasted three nights in the midst of drinking, exalted prayers, licentious songs, and lewd dances beside the "wine-colored sea". Saint Athanasius describes it as "the deification of luxury". Pancasta, the mistress of Alexander the Great, posed for Apelles, who painted her as Venus Anadyomene, or Venus "rising from the sea". En route to a war that he was waging against the Jews, Titus, like other famous personages, stopped here for a pilgrimage to the sacred temple of the goddess.

At Paphos our missionaries had to contend with a theosophist magician (and there were quite a few of them at the time). Named Bar-Jesus, and known also by the name of Elymas, he had won the confidence of the proconsul Sergius Paulus. Such characters were often part of the entourage of rich Romans. Pompey and Caesar, along with most of their contemporaries, were very superstitious and often consulted soothsayers, astrologers, or other diviners. One of them warned Caesar to "beware the ides of March". Juvenal ridicules Tiberius seated on the rock of Capri, in the midst of his "flock of Chaldeans and sorcerers". Pliny informs us that there were two schools of that sort in Paphos, one Jewish and the other Cypriot.

Sergius Paulus is described as a *synetos*, or "prudent" man, in Acts. Like many cultivated Romans of his time, he was deeply disappointed in the religion and philosophy of his time; he was seeking something else to appease his thirst for true spirituality. Bar-Jesus could not satisfy it, and when he heard about Barnabas and Paul, he invited them to his residence to find out what they had to say. Worried about his influence and his future, Bar-Jesus opposed the missionaries, trying with all his might to drive them away from the proconsul.

Then "Saul, who is also called Paul", filled with the Holy Spirit and incensed by this opposition, turned to Elymas:

> "You son of the devil, you enemy of all righteousness, full of all deceit and villainy, will you not stop making crooked the straight paths of the Lord? And now, behold, the hand

of the Lord is upon you, and you shall be blind and unable
to see the sun for a time." Immediately mist and darkness
fell upon him and he went about seeking people to lead
him by the hand. (Acts 13:9–11)

After witnessing the scene, the proconsul embraced the
faith, eager to hear the word of the Lord. A convert? If
so, what a convert! One soul is equal to another, but an
important man who turns to the Lord can use his influence
for the glory of God. This was the first of Paul's battles
which, we hope, was crowned with success.

Christianity replaced the cult of Venus. We know that
a community of Christians was established very early at
Paphos, and Salamis became the principal see on Cyprus.
The Church of Christ has endured on that island through
all the vicissitudes of two thousand years of history.

After completing his service on Cyprus, Sergius Paulus was appointed commissioner of the Tiber under the
emperor Claudius in 47; this is noted on a cippus, or funeral
column, that was discovered on the Via Giulia in 1887.

Antioch of Pisidia

From Paphos, Paul and Barnabas (still accompanied by
Mark) set sail for Attaleia, a crossing of 170 miles. Attaleia
was the place where the Athenian Cimon conquered the
Persians on land and on the sea in 416 B.C. and where the
combined squadrons of Rome and Rhodes annihilated
the fleet of Antiochus, with the terrible Hannibal on board,
in 190 B.C.

Paul and his companions ascended the river Caestrus,
or Kestrus, as far as Perga, the capital of Pamphylia, where
the famous temple of Diana crowned the hill behind
the city, magnificently silhouetted against a blue background. Attaleia was the place where John Mark deserted

the missionary party and returned to Jerusalem. Paul and Barnabas pushed on through the uncivilized mountains of the country (still a wilderness) until they reached the high plateau that forms the largest region in the interior of present-day Turkey. On the third or fourth day they arrived at Adada, located in the middle of an immense forest. Through a narrow, precipitous pass they emerged at what is today Lake Egridir, a lake some thirty miles in length, filled with limpid mountain waters and containing islands inhabited by countless wild swans and storks. They finally arrived at the little town of Neapolis and, after marching twenty miles by a Roman road, reached Antioch of Pisidia (near the present town of Yalvatch), located one hundred miles inland, as the crow flies, at an altitude of thirty-nine hundred feet above sea level.

After the battle of Magnesia in 190 B.C., in which Antiochus the Great lost all his territories located north of Taurus, the Romans made Antioch of Pisidia a free city. In 39 B.C. Mark Antony offered it to Amyntas, upon whose death, fifteen years later, it became a city in the vast province of Galatia. Around A.D. 6, Augustus transformed it into a Roman colony and made it the center of the southern part of that province. The ruins of white marble temples, of churches, of a theater, and of an aqueduct still testify today to the ancient splendor of the city. It was a center of the trade in animal skins and the fabric woven from long goat hair. The worship of Men, the lunar deity, was celebrated in the midst of orgies that were so vile and vicious that even the Romans were offended by them; they put an end to them by ordering the banishment of the priests, the priestesses, and the *hierodouloi*, slaves that served in the temple.

Not far from there the army of Cyrus mutinied for five days to obtain a pay raise. After a trying march across

Phrygia, the Crusaders, under the command of Bohemond of Tarentum and [his nephew] Tancred, were finally able to find some rest at Antioch.

Let us return to our travelers. No doubt they met with an offer of lodgings and even work in the "foreigners' rooms" that every important synagogue had to offer to coreligionists who were passing through. On the first Sabbath, Paul and Barnabas went to the synagogue. In their respective capacities as rabbi and Levite, they were led to the seats reserved for the "guests of honor" before the Ark containing the sacred scrolls of the Law. Therefore they were facing the people. After the religious service, the synagogue leaders turned to them: "Brethren, if you have any word of exhortation for the people, say it" (Acts 13:15). Paul did not hesitate; raising his hand as a sign of salutation, he pronounced the first sermon that we have by him on record.

The assembly was made up of the "children of Israel", Jews by birth, and of Gentiles who had become Jews by circumcision, all of them full members of the synagogue. Present also were the "God-fearing men", *theon sebomenoi*, pagans who were very interested in the Jewish religion but, in the men's case, had not yet taken the step of circumcision.

After a short introduction, Paul began: "Men of Israel, and you that fear God, listen" (Acts 13:16).

Historical section. God chose Israel. He chose and formed it for the sole purpose of preparing the world for the coming of Jesus, the Messiah. This Jesus was crucified, died, was buried, and rose again according to the promise made to the prophets. He is the Messiah, the long-awaited Savior.

Doctrinal section. You cannot be justified by the Law of Moses alone. You have all fallen short of the Law, and there is no justification in the works of the Law.

Only in Christ and through Christ are all those justified who believed in him. Christ was put to death for our
offenses. He sacrificed himself for us so as to make us just
in God's sight.

All who believe will be justified. This is the perfect work
of Christ, a gratuitous gift that can be neither purchased
nor merited.

Paul's speech was expressed plainly and simply, but it
was so revolutionary that it was not understood very well
by the assembly. "As they went out, the people begged
that these things might be told them [again] the next
sabbath" (Acts 13:42). However, a number of Jews and
proselytes followed Paul and Barnabas, and the latter
spoke to the locals, urging them to remain faithful to
the grace of God.

"When the Jews saw the multitudes, they were filled
with jealousy, and contradicted what was spoken by Paul,
and reviled him" (13:45). Denunciation and ridicule are not
reasonable persuasion. This was true in Paul's time and it is
still true today. "And Paul and Barnabas spoke out boldly,
saying, 'It was necessary that the word of God should be
spoken first to you. Since you thrust it from you, and judge
yourselves unworthy of eternal life, behold, we turn to the
Gentiles" (13:46).

There was something new in the air. Until then the
Gentiles had been brought to God by way of the synagogue; henceforth they would come directly to Jesus, without passing through the vestibule of Judaism. As Paul says,
God "had opened a door of faith to the Gentiles" (14:27).
We are witnessing here a momentous turning point in the
history of the world: the beginning of the systematic proclamation of Christianity to the Gentiles.

The Jews did not consider themselves defeated. They
incited the aristocratic women and the leading men of the

city. They organized a persecution against Paul and Barnabas and drove them out of the city. Were they perhaps
beaten with rods? (see 2 Cor 11:25). Our missionaries shook
the dust from their sandals in protest and set out on the
road to Iconium.

The work of Paul and Barnabas in Antioch of Pisidia
was not without results. That remote province eventually
had twenty-five suffragan bishops in the Metropolitan See of
Antioch. They sent missionaries to Cappadocia, the neighboring province, which in turn produced a great number of
illustrious men who dominated the fourth Christian century.
Among them were the distinguished Basil the Great, his
brother Gregory of Nyssa, and Gregory of Nazianzus, "the
Theologian", who was a fellow student of Julian the Apostate,
became the patriarch of Constantinople, and wrote prose
that has been described as "angelic". Around the year 300
we find that Eudoxius of Antioch was martyred during the
persecution of Diocletian, along with Marcus, Alphius, and
others. In 314 Sergianos was the delegate from the Antio-
chene community to the Council of Ancyra, and in 325
Antonius participated in the important Council of Nicaea.

Iconium

Our missionaries directed their steps toward the southeast,
taking an excellent road that led to Iconium, around 110
miles away. En route they crossed arid plains, surrounded
by pestilential marshes, where gaunt flocks of goats, sheep,
donkeys, and wild asses grazed. At last they reached a large
oasis that enclosed, as though in a gold and chrysoprase
jewel box, the pretty town of Iconium (today Konya), at an
altitude of more than thirty-three hundred feet above sea
level. An important crossroads on the imperial Via Sebaste,
located between Ephesus and Tarsus, it was nestled between

snow-covered mountains to the east and the vast plain with its enormous lake to the west.

According to the legend, Nannakos was king of Iconium at the time of the Great Deluge. Jupiter then ordered Prometheus to fashion images or "icons" of clay representing human beings, over which he made the wind blow so as to give them life and replace the men drowned in the flood waters. From these icons the name of the city is said to have been derived: Iconium.

Xenophon stopped at Iconium with his band of ten thousand Greek adventurers in 349 B.C., at the beginning of his famous retreat and expedition, which he recounts in his work *Anabasis*. In the year 51 B.C., Cicero stayed there en route to Tarsus, where he would occupy the position of governor of Cilicia. Around A.D. 47–48, Paul came to Iconium for a much more famous expedition.

Paul and Barnabas went to the synagogue to announce the good news. They did this in a way that was so convincing "that a great company believed, both of Jews and of Greeks" (Acts 14:1). They stayed for some time in the city, bearing witness to the Lord and to his grace by the signs and miracles that were worked at their hands. But the city was divided. On the one side were Paul and Barnabas and their group of converts, and on the other side were the Jews. And when a faction of leading Jews and pagans had formed with the intention of seizing the missionaries and stoning them, the latter were informed about the plan and they left the city without delay.

It is said that the famous Thecla was converted by Paul at Iconium. The "Acts of Paul and Thecla", based on a very ancient document, describe Paul for us as "a short, bowlegged man, with a receding hairline, a stout build, a prominent nose and eyebrows that met. A creature full of grace, who sometimes resembled a man and at other times had the appearance of an angel." This description comes from a hagiographic [as opposed to an historical] source, but it is important because it was the basis for many portraits, some of which go back to the earliest Christian centuries. I did not want to follow that tradition; I preferred to use on the cover of this book a less conventional but perhaps more accurate image of the apostle that comes from the hypogeum, the underground burial chamber, of the Aurelii in Rome.

Over the following centuries, until the Turkish conquest, Iconium was one of the important centers of Christianity in the region. Hierax, a slave of Iconium and friend of Justin Martyr, was executed in Rome in the year 168 for being a Christian. In 235 a council was held in the city, and in 371 the local bishop, Amphilocus, was noted for his zeal and holiness. We know that there were sixteen episcopal sees in Lycaonia around the year 300. Frederick Barbarossa, on his way to liberating the Holy Land, arrived at the gates of Iconium in 1190. Thanks to his heroism, he won a decisive battle and captured the city. He then ordered a Mass of thanksgiving for all the Crusaders and asked the bishop of Mayence to preach on the text of Acts 13:51: Paul and Barnabas "shook off the dust from their feet against them, and went to Iconium." *Venerunt Iconium.*

The Seljukians, the manliest and most artistic of all the Turkish tribes, made Iconium the capital of their empire, Roum. They transformed it, making it so beautiful that it became a proverb: "Discover the world: visit Konya." Located there was the tomb of Tekke of Mevla, who discovered in the Bible that David had danced in the presence of the Lord and who started to dance also as a form of prayer; he subsequently founded the sect of the whirling dervishes. At his death he was buried standing and his tomb was covered with a gold veil.

Lystra

Ovid tells us that Lycaon did not believe in the gods, and to punish him he was transformed into a wolf (*lycos* in Greek), whence the name of the region: Lycaonia. There Zeus and Hermes came down to earth and knocked in vain at many doors, but no one offered them hospitality. They were welcomed in the humble dwelling of Philemon and Baucis. In return, their poor hovel was transformed into a magnificent temple, of which they became the ministers. When the great flood came and the human race perished by drowning, Philemon was metamorphosed into a majestic oak and Baucis into a graceful linden tree (see Ovid, *Metamorphoses*, 8, 626).

Despite their harsh experience, Paul and Barnabas turned to the south, in the direction of Lystra, situated about nineteen miles from Iconium. Since the year 6 B.C., this little city at an altitude of thirty-nine hundred feet had been a Roman colony, snuggled in a peaceful valley in the middle of a magnificent mountain landscape.   The city has disappeared, but investigations in the nineteenth century led to the rediscovery of some ruins not far from present-day Hatunsaray.

At Lystra there was a lame man who had never been able to walk. He heard about Paul and came to listen to him. He watched him with such intensity that Paul could tell that he had the faith and the desire to be healed. He said to him in a loud voice, "Get up and walk!" (see Acts 14:10). And the paralytic stood up and began to walk.

When the people realized what Paul had just done, they exclaimed in the Lycaonian dialect, "The gods have come down to us in the likeness of men!" (14:11). They supposed that Barnabas was Zeus and that Paul, the main speaker, must be Hermes. Indeed, they knew that it was beneath the dignity of a god to converse with human beings, and so that was left to an inferior god.

The priest of Zeus, whose temple loomed at the city gates, when informed of the incident, hurried to bring bulls crowned with garlands so as to sacrifice them to the gods who had just appeared.

Upon learning this, Paul and Barnabas tore their garments to express their dismay and opposition, and dashing into the crowd, they exclaimed,

> [Friends,] why are you doing this? We also are men, of like nature with you, and bring you good news, that you should turn from these vain things to a living God who made the heaven and the earth and the sea and all that is in them. In past generations he allowed all the nations to walk in their own ways; yet he did not leave himself without witness, for he did good and gave you from heaven rains and fruitful seasons, satisfying your hearts with food and gladness. (14:15–17)

The crowd murmured, unhappy to find that the missionaries were denying them a holiday and, no doubt, a delectable banquet. And when certain Jews from Antioch and Iconium arrived to whisper their calumnies in the ears of these uncouth provincials, they persuaded them quickly enough to stone those mysterious strangers. Dragging Paul outside the city, they pelted him with stones and left him for dead. But when the disciples drew near to pay their last respects, he suddenly stood up and went back into the city.

Was it in the house of Eunice and Lois that Paul's wounds were treated? These Jewish women were converted at Lystra with their son and grandson, respectively, Timothy. Later on Paul would address the latter as "my true child in the faith" (1 Tim 1:2). Timothy no doubt witnessed the stoning, because Paul writes, "Now you have observed...my persecutions, my sufferings, what befell me at Antioch, at Iconium, and at Lystra, what persecutions I endured; yet from them all the Lord rescued me" (2 Tim 3:10–11).

Cicero stayed in that region for several weeks and speaks about the people there as a savage, treacherous, and inconstant race. Aristotle notes that the Lycaonians were not trustworthy.

Eustochius paid a visit to his parents in Lystra, was arrested, brought to Ancyra, and condemned to death for having converted to Christianity. Tiberius was bishop of Lystra when he participated in the Council of Nicaea in 325. Paul of Lystra is mentioned at the Council of Constaninople in 381.

Derbe

As soon as he had recovered from his wounds, Paul left the city by the Via Sebaste, the imperial road that had been restored in A.D. 6 by Publius Sulpicius Quirinus, governor of Syria. Our two missionaries set out for Derbe, ninety-nine miles away. It was a frontier fortress and a toll house where the brigand Antipater welcomed Cicero with all the honors due to that dangerous Roman.

At Derbe, Paul and Barnabas had the joy of making several conversions and many friends. We know that Gaius of Derbe was with Paul during his last visit to Jerusalem (see Acts 20:4).

When the apostles had ordained the *presbyteroi*, "elders", by the imposition of hands in each of the churches that they founded, and after fasting and praying, they commended them to the Lord in whom they now believed. Paul and Barnabas then took the return route, retracing their steps via Pisidia to Pamphylia. They made the Lord known in Perga and then covered the ten miles that separated them from

Attaleia (modern Antalya). This city had been founded by
Attalus Philadelphus, king of Pergamum (150–138 B.C.) at
the mouth of the Katarrhaktes, which traces out its path
to the sea by a series of cataracts or waterfalls, which give
the river its name.

From that Pamphylian port our voyagers set sail for Seleucia, beheld the pointed cone of Mount Casius, and followed
the course of the Orontes upstream in the midst of green
oaks, strawberry trees [*Arbutus unedo*], and myrtles. They
did not fail to glance at the sinister face of Charon sculpted
on the side of the mountain, and finally they crossed the
bridge leading back to Singon Street. The Christians there
welcomed them effusively. And when they gathered in the
place which custom already called the *ekklesia* [church],
they gave thanks to the Lord for all that the two missionaries had accomplished and for having opened up the way
of the faith to the Gentiles.

Thus Paul's first missionary journey came to an end.
After that long and perilous voyage of almost 680 miles,
Paul and Barnabas stayed for a long time with the Chris-
tians of Antioch; they needed the rest.

The Assembly of Jerusalem

The Judaizing Christians of Jerusalem demanded that Gentile converts comply with all the precepts of the Law of
Moses, including circumcision. Paul and the brethren of
Antioch rejected those strict conditions, and in order to
clarify the matter, they decided to send Paul and Barnabas
to Jerusalem to confer with the apostles and the elders.
The Acts of the Apostles tells us that "they passed through
both Phoenicia and Samaria, reporting the conversion of
the Gentiles, and they gave great joy to all the brethren.
When they came to Jerusalem, they were welcomed by the

Church and the apostles and the elders, and they declared all that God had done with them" [Acts 15:3–4].

The discussion was lively, but finally Peter stood up and said, "Brethren, you know that in the early days [at the time of the conversion of the pagan Cornelius] God made choice among you, that by my mouth the Gentiles should hear the word of the gospel and believe. And God who knows the heart bore witness to them, giving them the Holy Spirit just as he did to us" (Acts 15:7–8). Peter then recalled Christ's words (see Mt 23:4) concerning the burdensome observances of the Law "which neither our fathers nor we have been able to bear" (Acts 15:10).

A great silence fell over the assembly. Then they listened to Paul and Barnabas, who explained all the miracles and marvels that God had accomplished through them among the pagans.

When they had finished speaking, James, the relative of Jesus, nicknamed "the Just" because of his great sanctity, quoted Amos 9:11–12 to show how the New Way is the fulfillment of Judaism; it was his judgment, therefore, "that we should not trouble those of the Gentiles who turn to God" (Acts 15:19). They should simply abstain from foods sacrificed to idols, from all fornication, from the meat of strangled animals, and from blood.

The Report Sent to Antioch

The speeches by Peter and James pleased the apostles, the elders, and the whole Church. A delegation was sent to Antioch to inform the brethren of the results of the assembly, of what was in fact the first council of the Christian Church. The delegation was made up of Judas called Barsabbas and Silas, an eminent person among the brethren in Jerusalem.

Not content with a verbal report, the assembly composed
and sent a letter that is said to be the most ancient document
in the history of the Church; it is recorded in the Acts of
the Apostles 15:23–29 and is worth citing in its entirety.

> The brethren, both the apostles and the elders, to the
> brethren who are of the Gentiles in Antioch and Syria and
> Cilicia, greeting.
>
> Since we have heard that some persons from us have
> troubled you with words, unsettling your minds, although
> we gave them no instructions, it has seemed good to us in
> assembly to choose men and send them to you with our
> beloved Barnabas and Paul, men who have risked their lives
> for the sake of our Lord Jesus Christ. We have therefore
> sent Judas and Silas, who themselves will tell you the same
> things by word of mouth.
>
> For it has seemed good to the Holy Spirit and to us
> to lay upon you no greater burden than these necessary
> things: that you abstain from what has been sacrificed to
> idols and from blood and from what is strangled and from
> unchastity. If you keep yourselves from these, you will do
> well. Farewell. [*Érrōsthe*].

The delegates left Jerusalem for Antioch, and when they
had arrived among the people of God, they delivered the
letter from the apostles and strengthened them in their
faith. Finally, after spending some time in Antioch, the
brethren sent them back in peace to the apostles of Jerusalem, but Silas saw fit to stay in Antioch. Paul and Barnabas
continued their work among the inhabitants of the city,
"teaching and preaching the word of the Lord" (Acts 15:35).

It may seem astonishing to read that the letter cautions
the brethren against all sorts of unchastity. The fact is that,
at the beginning of the Christian era, even the rabbis had
rather loose morals, and among the pagans fornication was
often part of the religious practice in the temples of their

idols. Socrates does not condemn it; Terence and Horace see nothing in it to find fault with; Cato the Censor, the model of Roman *virtus*, was guilty of it. All this shows the beneficial influence that the pure gospel of Christ had in the pagan world, from the very beginning.

The debate in Jerusalem was the first great crisis that the New Way had to face. Fortunately, through the action of the Holy Spirit working through Peter, James, Paul, and all the apostles and elders, Christianity emerged from its Jewish chrysalis and metamorphosed into a universal religion.

Saint Peter in Antioch

Shortly after the council, no doubt in order to become better acquainted with that Church composed mainly of Gentile converts, which was so vibrant and so militant, Peter decided to pay it a visit. He was welcomed with joy, respect, and the best hospitality. He conversed with them, shared their meals, took part in their prayers, spoke to them about Jesus, whom he had known during his earthly life, and presided at their celebrations of the Eucharist.

Everything was going very well until the arrival of certain persons sent by the Judaizers, who began to criticize Peter, declaring that "unless you are circumcised according to the custom of Moses, you cannot be saved" (Acts 15:1). Peter then separated himself from the Gentile Christians, for fear of the circumcision party. "And with him the rest of the Jews acted insincerely, so that even Barnabas was carried away by their insincerity" (Gal 2:13).

Paul responded sharply and without hesitation. He confronted Peter and spoke to him with all the fire that we know he was capable of. "But when Cephas came to Antioch I opposed him to his face, because he stood condemned" (Gal 2:11).

Paul used to recommend patience and understanding for the Christians of Jewish origin who continued to keep certain observances, such as fast days and foods prepared according to the dietary laws of the Mosaic Law. But on the crucial point of the freedom of Christians with regard to the Law, the apostle of the Gentiles always maintained a firm, unambiguous position, recalling, when the need arose, the decisions of the assembly of Jerusalem. In no way was Paul's correction an attack on Peter's authority. Quite to the contrary! If someone else had acted in that manner, Paul would have let the incident go without comment. But it was a question of the attitude of Cephas, the rock of the Church! Paul had the duty to react firmly so as not to give the impression that Christians had to accept and follow the Mosaic Law.

Far from diminishing the unity of the Church, this episode demonstrates the great spiritual solidarity that reigned among the apostles: the deference of Paul toward the visible head of the Church and the humility of Peter who corrected his own behavior.

6

The Second Missionary Journey I:
Philippi, Thessalonica, Beroea

"Come, let us return and visit the brethren in every city where we proclaimed the word of the Lord, and see how they are", said Paul (Acts 15:36). Barnabas agreed but wanted to be accompanied by his cousin John, called Mark, who asked to rejoin their little band. But Paul refused outright to take along the one who had left them in Pamphylia, refusing his share of the work.

The discussion on this subject was very lively and ended with a complete separation between the two missionaries. Accompanied by Mark, Barnabas set sail for Cyprus. This is the last time he is mentioned in the New Testament. Tradition tells us that he was burned alive at Salamis, where a church and a grotto are named after him.

Mark had abandoned them during their first journey, and Paul did not want to take the risk of compromising the second mission with such an unreliable collaborator. This was a difference in prudential judgment between Paul and Barnabas as to their method of working, and not a problem of doctrine or a personal conflict.

The encouragement offered by Barnabas and the firm decision reached by Paul made Mark a man who later on courageously enlisted in the service of the latter. The apostle Peter mentions him as a faithful co-worker. Later on the Spirit would lead him to write the Gospel according to Saint Mark, and Paul notes in 2 Timothy 4:11, "He is profitable to me for the ministry" (Douay-Rheims).

Paul chose Silas, also called Silvanus, as his traveling companion and, placing the mission in God's hands, set out on his journey with the blessing of the brethren. On their departure from Antioch, walking due north and ascending the valley of the Orontes, they crossed the plain where, later on, the troops of Zenobia, queen of Palmyra, were defeated by the Roman legions. Taken prisoner and brought to Rome, she was the trophy in the triumph of Aurelianus in 273. After crossing the mountains of Amanus by the Syrian Gates, they entered the vast plain of the Cilicia Campestris. In 333 B.C. this had been the site of the famous Battle of Issus, where Alexander Aniketos (the Invincible) conquered the Persian king Darius Codomanus, who handed Syria and the Orient over to the young Macedonian.

Our three travelers skirted the Gulf of Issus, passed the market town of Aegae near the present-day city of Ceyhan, then Mopsuestia, the "home of Mopsus", where the famous Theodore was bishop for thirty-six years and died in 428. They soon reached Adana and then Tarsus, which is 155 miles distant from Antioch and 512 miles northwest of Jerusalem. It seems that they did not linger in Paul's birthplace but rather pushed on in the direction of Mopsukrenè, the "fountain of Mopsus", and passed through the formidable Gates of Cilicia in the mountains of Taurus, at an altitude of more than 3,280 feet.

Xenophon (third century B.C.) described these gates for us: "Between two walls flows the Carsus River, which is around 100 feet wide. The entire space running between the walls is not quite three stadia long (one-third mile), and it is impossible to take it by storm, because the passage is

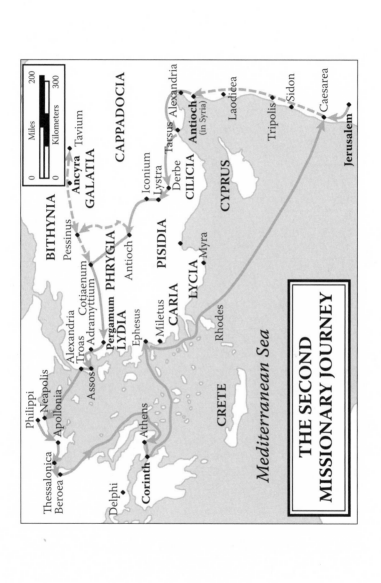

THE SECOND
MISSIONARY JOURNEY

too narrow, there is a sheer drop from the mountains into the sea, and the rocks on the heights prove impassable."

Our little band, no doubt in the company of other travelers for safety's sake, then continued its march along the Via Sebaste in a northwesterly direction toward Derbe and Lystra. There they were joyfully welcomed by Eunice, her son Timothy, and Lois, his grandmother. From his earliest youth Timothy had been educated in the Jewish religion (see 2 Tim 1:5). His father was a Gentile, but his entire education had been entrusted to his mother and his grandmother. We know that they had met Paul and were conquered by the Word of the Lord. They had also witnessed the persecutions that the apostle had suffered, which are reported in 2 Timothy 3:11–15. When does the education of a child begin? "Twenty years before his birth through the mother's education", popular wisdom tells us.

Timothy had a good reputation among the brethren of Lystra and Iconium (see Acts 16:1–2). Paul, who was looking for a close collaborator, succeeded in convincing Eunice and Lois—which no doubt was not easy—to allow him to take Timothy with him in the service of the Lord. So as not to offend the Jews and the Judaizing party, he had him circumcised. Then he proceeded to ordain him and, by the imposition of hands, made him a coadjutor in the Lord's vineyard.

Timothy was faithful to Paul to the end. He helped him to spread the Gospel "as a son with a father" (Phil 2:22); they were so completely of one mind that "I have no one like him" (Phil 2:20; see 1 Tim 1:2).

The missionaries went from city to city in the province of Galatia, implementing the decisions of the Council of Jerusalem. Thus the faithful of the local churches were strengthened in the faith, and their number increased day by day.

"And they went through the region of Phrygia and Galatia, having been forbidden by the Holy Spirit to speak the word in [the Roman province of] Asia" (Acts 16:6). Upon their arrival in the regions of Mysia, they attempted to go into Bithynia, but the Spirit did not allow them. Why not? Maybe because the apostle Peter had preached there. The gospel had been proclaimed very early in Bithynia, with the greatest possible success. Pliny the Younger, governor of Bithynia and Pontus in 112, wrote from Amisus (today Amasra) on the Black Sea his letters, numbered 96 and 97, addressed to the emperor Trajan. In them he reported that Christianity had spread everywhere, that the temples were abandoned, and the sacrifices discontinued.

Paul and his companions took the road to Mysia, no doubt passing through Apamea, Laodicea, Philadelphia, Sardis, Thyatira, Pergamum, and Adramyttium, to arrive at Troas of Alexandria, which at that time was both a port and a Roman colony situated nine miles from ancient Troy.

There Alexander the Great strengthened his resolve at the tomb of Achilles and then, reinvigorated, went on to conquer the Orient. There, too, Julius Caesar, after the battle of Pharsalus, dreamed of establishing the capital of the Roman world. Here also, Herod Atticus brought pure, fresh running water from Mount Ida, as the pillars of his aqueduct still testify today. Much later, in the nineteenth century, Heinrich Schliemann spent a fortune to discover not one city of Troy but at least nine, one on top of the other; Troy VIIa seems to be the one from Homer's epic.

Philippi

Troas. Troy! What grandeur it evokes! Did Paul have some sense of its glorious past? We know that he had a vision: "A man of Macedonia was standing pleading with him and saying, 'Come over to Macedonia and help us.' And when he had seen the vision, immediately we sought to go on into Macedonia" (Acts 16:9–10). Notice the words "him" and "we". It seems that Luke, the physician and great traveler, who probably was originally from Antioch, had joined Paul at Troas and remained to the end his most faithful collaborator.

The Mediterranean has almost no tide; its entire eastern coast is sprinkled with islands, promontories, and peninsulas. The sea is rather calm in the summer, a constant encouragement for the mariner and most travelers. Along with the Phoenicians, it was the ancient Greeks who, over long centuries, established the basis for the nautical knowledge of the Greco-Roman world.

In the ancient world, the season for sailing extended from March to October, when visibility was good and allowed navigation by the stars and the calm sea. At the first sign of bad weather or storms, a boat took refuge in an emergency harbor or in a little port that was well shielded from the waves. The sea crossing from Alexandria Troas in Asia to Neapolis in Thrace is short, about 136 miles. The traveler had to use a cargo ship, *navis oneraria*, with a capacity of about fifty-five short tons, or a coasting vessel of even smaller tonnage. These ships were very slow, traveling at three to five knots (three to five nautical miles per hour), depending on the wind. (A nautical mile equals 6,080 feet.)

With a tailwind and favorable weather, the boat that carried Paul and his assistants labored for some time against the powerful current that rushes past Hellespont, the Dardanelles of today, then steered for the islands of Tenedos and Imbros. Under the deep waters that separate the two islands, according to Greek mythology, was the cave of Neptune, the god of the ocean. To the left the passengers descried Lemnos, where Vulcan the blacksmith disembarked, driven from heaven by the enraged Zeus, his father. Located here too was the cave of Morpheus, the god of sleep and half brother of death. Later Jason and his Argonauts would repopulate the island.

Our missionaries were able to rest a while in the calm waters of that island, which was protected by the island of Samothrace, from which Jupiter watched the battles of the Trojan War. On Lemnos also many sailors were initiated into the mysteries of Kabiri, Phoenician deities that protected mariners against shipwreck.

Very early in the morning they went to sea again, and by the end of the day they had rounded the island of Thasos, the native place of the painter Polygnotus, who invented the technique for painting transparent draperies. They observed the rocky outcroppings of Mount Pangaeus, discovered a far-flung ridge crowned with a temple, and set foot on land at Neapolis, "the new city", in the province of Thrace, in Europe. This was the port of Philippi, in Macedonia, situated about ten miles from Neapolis. They covered this final stretch, on foot, in a few hours. On their return, the sea voyage lasted five days (see Acts 20:6), no doubt to allow for stops at Thasos, Samothrace, and Lemnos, or because of unfavorable winds.

The ruins of an aqueduct and the remains of a military road can still be seen at Neapolis. The little group left the city by the eastern gate and took the famous Via Egnatia, which begins at that locality. Walking farther north, they passed the lesser mountain chain alongside Mount Pangaeus. In front of them stretched the vast plain of Philippi.

Farther on they were able to admire the massive Mount Pangaeus in all its splendor: the sacred mountain dedicated to Dionysius, the Greek Bacchus. There the disheveled, demented priestesses of the temple indulged in lascivious dances during orgies that swiftly turned violent, one of the most malignant aspects of paganism. The mountain, covered with forests, was rich in gold and silver. Philip of Macedon extracted from it each year more than a thousand talents of gold, an enormous sum that financed the famous Macedonian phalanx, with the help of which Alexander the Great conquered the world. At the foot of that mountain flowed the Crenides, the "Fountains" that gave their name to the city, which subsequently was changed to Philippi.

At Sardis, the capital of the kingdom of Lydia, which was made famous by its king Croesus, the ghost of Caesar had said to Brutus, "I will meet you again at Philippi", as Plutarch records and William Shakespeare dramatizes for us. Brutus went to Philippi with Cassius to wage war on Octavius and Antony, a fatal encounter that sounded the death knell of the Roman Republic and paved the way for the establishment of the empire under Octavius, who became Caesar Augustus in 27 B.C. It was during that battle that the poet Horace, on the losing side, seeing their fortunes turn, "tossed his little round shield aside and fled quickly", "*et celerem fugam sensi, relicta non bene parmula*".

To celebrate his victory, Octavius had a triumphal arch erected on the banks of the Gangites, outside of Philippi, which was transformed into a Roman colony. These colonies were a pale imitation of Rome, lost in the immensity of the empire, but a Rome despite it all. The colonists had their names inscribed in the registers of one or another Roman tribe, which gave them the right to vote; the military flags were flown in the city; the *Lex Romana* [Roman law] was in force; Latin was spoken there and was found also on the coins struck in the region. The laws of the Twelve Tables were inscribed on bronze tablets, aere perennius, which were posted in the Forum.

More than a hundred years later another battle was fought at Philippi and another victory was won, but this time with the sword of the Spirit of God. At the place where the dying Brutus had pronounced his last words, "May the gods take revenge on the enemies of Rome for these many misfortunes", Paul preached the good news, which taught people to pray for their enemies. Here, Paul had the joy of receiving his first convert on European soil.

On the Sabbath following their arrival, Paul, Silas, and Timothy went to the banks of the Gangites River outside the city to pray in a *proseucha* (*proseuchè*, "prayer", in Greek). It was a flimsy building, often with no roof. In places where there was no synagogue the Jews often gathered near flowing water, which facilitated their ritual purifications.

"We sat down and spoke to the women who had come together" (Acts 16:13). One of them, named Lydia, was a seller of purple goods originally from the city of Thyatira. Already in Homer's time the province of Lydia was highly renowned for the quality of its dyes, especially purple. Lydia was a *sebomènè*, someone who feared and worshipped God. Her heart was open to everything that Paul said, and after being baptized along with her entire household, she extended an invitation to the missionaries in these words: " 'If you have judged me to be faithful to the Lord, come to my house and stay.' And she prevailed upon us". (Acts 16:15).

Lydia must have been one of those strong women who are used to commanding obedience, without discussion.

On another occasion, when Paul and his companions were going to the place of prayer, they were met by a slave girl (*paidíka* in Greek) who was possessed by an evil spirit. It was a "pythonical" spirit that could predict the future, and she thereby earned a lot of money for her owners. Python in Greek mythology was the serpent who guarded the famous oracle of Delphi and was killed by Apollo.

In those days even the most famous and best educated pagans were extremely superstitious; they sought advice about all sorts of problems in their daily lives from oracles, soothsayers, fortune-tellers, seers, astrologers, magicians, and other charlatans who were paid royally. The oracle of Delphi had been considerably enriched by the practice. We know that the Phoenicians of Anatolia one day seized its treasury, which had an incalculable value.

The girl with the spirit of divination followed Paul and his companions everywhere they went, crying, "These men are servants of the Most High God, who proclaim to you the way of salvation" (Acts 16:17). She treated them as very important persons, announcing their arrival and their mission. She used the Greek word *hupsístos*, "most high", which was an epithet applied to Zeus, and this pagan connotation must not have pleased Paul at all. She made the same scene repeatedly for several days in a row. The fiery-tempered Paul soon had had enough, and he said to the evil spirit, "I charge you in the name of Jesus Christ to come out of her" (16:18). And the spirit left her that very hour.

When her owners realized that their hope of a significant income was gone, they seized Paul and Silas and dragged them to the Forum, claiming, "These men are Jews and they are disturbing our city. They advocate customs which it is not lawful for us Romans to accept or practice" (16:20–21).

What is playing itself out here is the first persecution of Paul by the pagans. The allurement of profit and not respect for the Roman religion was the motive for their accusation. Knowing that the magistrates could not allow an appeal to the courts of justice for damages and interests, the owners of the slave girl very shrewdly accused the missionaries of propagating a new religion. Roman law permitted the Jews to practice their religion, but Roman citizens were formally forbidden to undergo circumcision under pain of serious consequences, as Livy attests.

The phrase "These men are Jews" was very astutely introduced to remind the Roman judges that the emperor Claudius had just banished that plague-ridden race from Rome and that they therefore had no right to any clemency. The Roman colony of Philippi, surely, would have to follow the example set by Rome.

The rabble was roused against Paul and Silas, and the intimidated "magistrates tore the garments off them and gave orders to beat them with rods" (Acts 16:22). Once that was done, they were thrown into prison with the assurance that the jailer would keep strict guard over them. The latter locked them in the deepest dungeon and fastened their feet in the stocks, a humiliating and painful treatment.

The question arises: To avoid the beating, why didn't Paul claim his status as a Roman citizen? He probably knew that it would not do any good. The crowd was threatening and the officials were in too much of a hurry to avoid a riot. Cicero tells us that in the middle of the Forum of Messina, in Sicily, the victim of Verres shouted in vain during a whipping, "I am a Roman citizen."

The Gospel of Matthew teaches us: "Blessed are you when men revile you and persecute you and utter all kinds of evil against you falsely on my account" (5:11). After Peter spent time in his prison, it was Paul's turn to witness for Christ. "About midnight Paul and Silas were praying and singing hymns to God, and the prisoners were listening to them" (Acts 16:25).

Songs of thanksgiving in a prison? There indeed is something new under the sun! Did Paul remember the passage from Job (35:10) "Where is God my Maker, who gives songs [of joy] in the night?" Suddenly there was an earthquake that shook the foundations of the prison. All the doors were opened by the thrust, and the prisoners' fetters were loosed. The prison guard, wakened with a jolt and discovering that the prison doors were open, concluded that the prisoners had fled; he drew his sword to put himself to death, since he was responsible for them and would have to pay with his life.

But Paul cried in a loud voice, "Do not harm yourself, for we are all here" (Acts 16:28). The guard quickly called for light, rushed in, and, trembling, fell at the feet of Paul and Silas. After bringing them out, he asked them, "'Men, what must I do to be saved?' And they said 'Believe in the Lord Jesus, and you will be saved, you and your household'" (16:30–31). At that very hour the guard took them into his house, dressed their wounds, and, without further ado, received baptism with his entire household. He then offered them a meal and rejoiced with his family that he had believed in God.

He had dressed their wounds; Paul and Silas washed his soul with the water of baptism. He had asked for light; they gave him the true Light. He delivered them from their chains; they freed him from the attachments that bound his soul. He offered them food for their bodies; they gave him food for his soul.

As day dawned, the magistrates ordered the lictors [Roman officers], "Let those men go." The guard announced the news to Paul: "The magistrates have sent to let you go; now therefore come out and go in peace. [*Poreúesthe en eirénè!*]" But Paul had not finished speaking; the blood boiled in his veins: "[What?!] They have beaten us publicly, uncondemned, men who are Roman citizens, and have thrown us into prison; and do they now cast us out secretly? No! let them come themselves and take us out." The officers reported this suggestion to their superiors, who were seized with fear upon learning about their status as Roman citizens (16:35–37).

They had got themselves into a fine pickle! "It is a crime to fetter a Roman citizen; it is a crime to flagellate him", Cicero tells us in his lawsuit against Verres. Both the *Lex Valeria* from 509 B.C. and the *Lex Porcia* dated 248 B.C. condemned this crime, and anyone guilty of it was to be punished with dismissal from office and even, in certain cases, the death penalty.

The *strategoí*, the Greek word used for the magistrates in this passage from Acts (16:35), came to apologize to the missionaries; they took them out of the prison and begged them to leave the city. Paul and Silas went to Lydia's house, paid a visit to the brethren to encourage them, and, without too much haste, left Philippi.

Thessalonica

They took the Via Egnatia and traveled about thirty miles to the place where the river Strymon traces an enormous curve enveloping the city of Amphipolis (whence the name, "around-city"). It was a major commercial city at the intersection of nine roads. Its former name, in fact, had been "Nine Roads". The surrounding pine forests supplied the masts for the Athenian fleet. In 422 B.C. the Athenian Cleon received orders to recapture Amphipolis for Athens. He was defeated and killed by Brasidas from Sparta. Thucydides was no more successful, and he was exiled for his trouble. In one of his greatest speeches opposing Philip of Macedon, Demosthenes describes Amphipolis as a very important city in the fight against Macedonia. Here too, after the defeat of Persia at Pydna, L. Aemilius Paulus declared the independence of Macedonia. But Paul is the one who brought it true freedom.

Early in the morning, Paul and his companions crossed the wooded mountain pass of Aulon and reached the valley of Arethousa, where the tomb of the great Greek dramatist Euripides is located. From there they could see the village of Stagira, the birthplace of Aristotle, the great philosopher and tutor of Alexander. After another thirty-mile walk they reached Apollonia. The next day the little group went through the pass leading to the peninsula of Chalcidice, skirting the cities of Olympias and Potidaea to the south and finally reaching the important city of Thessalonica after a journey of around one hundred miles from Philippi. Originally it was called Therma, or "Hot Springs". Rebuilt in 315 B.C. by Cassander, it was renamed Thessalonika in honor of his wife, the daughter of Philip of Macedon. The latter had named her to commemorate the battle won in Thessaly on the day of her birth. It was the first stronghold captured by Xerxes on European soil. Here too loomed the triumphal arch celebrating the victory of Caesar Augustus at Philippi. And in A.D. 44 it served as the residence of the Roman proconsul.

From the city one can admire majestic Mount Olympus, which rears its snow-covered head at an altitude of 8,860 feet. At the summit, Zeus (or Jupiter) convened in council all the gods of Greece and decided the future of men. Marcus Tullius Cicero stayed there for seven months, a melancholy exile, with Planctus the quaestor, "lost in the farthest parts of the Roman empire, forgotten by the gods, in the midst of snow and ice".

Thick woods at the foot of the mountain concealed the spring Pieria, near which the Muses were born and where Orpheus saw the light of day. Not far from Olympus, toward the southeast, looms Mount Ossa, separated from Olympus by a defile or very narrow valley called Tempe, or "Notch", made with a single blow by Neptune's trident, through which the river Peneus flows into the sea. In this rustic site Orpheus sang his melodies, and the enchanted trees led him in procession toward the gates of death that opened before him. In that place, too, the god Apollo atoned for having caused the death of Python, the enormous serpent, and there he plucked the branch that he planted near the spring of Castalia, producing the sacred laurel tree of the oracle of Delphi.

Paul had taken lodgings with the Jewish man named Jason, and so as not to be a burden on anyone he began to ply his trade as a tentmaker (see 1 Thess 2:9; 2 Thess 3:8). Famine prevailed in the region and the price of wheat had reached six times the normal price. Paul gratefully accepted the help sent by his friends in Philippi.

Following his custom, Paul went to the synagogue and, three Sabbaths in a row, discussed the Scriptures, showing how they proved that the Messiah had to suffer and rise again from the dead. He added, "This Jesus, whom I proclaim to you, is the Christ" (Acts 17:3). Some of his listeners were converted and joined the little group that formed around the two missionaries. The same thing happened with a good number of *sebomenoi*, "God-fearing men", as well as some aristocratic women.

They did not have to wait long for a reaction. Several Jews, furious, recruited some scoundrels and stirred up a riot. They invaded Jason's house, looking for Paul and Silas so as to bring them before an assembly of the people. Since they could not find them, they dragged Jason and several other brethren before the politarchs, or city authorities.

The crowd shouted, "These men who have turned the world upside down have come here also, and Jason has received them; and they are all acting against the decrees of Caesar, saying that there is another king, Jesus" (Acts 17:6–7). These words alarmed the magistrates, and they did not release Jason until after he had paid bail.

Without wasting any time, at nightfall the brethren had Paul and his companions depart for Beroea.

Beroea

"Piso", the prefect of Macedonia, "fled Thessalonica and secretly went to Beroea", Cicero tells us. Just like Paul. In 355, Pope Liberius was banished from Rome to Beroea. This city is located around thirty-seven miles to the south-west of Thessalonica, traveling on horseback along the river Astreus, at the foot of Mount Bermius, which is part of the massif of Olympus. After the battle of Pydna in 108 B.C., Beroea was the first Greek city to accept the Roman occupation. Pompey set up his winter quarters/barracks there in the year 50 B.C.

As soon as they arrived in Beroea, Paul and Silas went to the synagogue, where the Jews of the city, who were more open-minded than those of Thessalonica, gladly welcomed the Word and examined the Scriptures each day to make sure that the new teaching was consistent with them. And many believed, among whom were Greeks, some women of high standing, and a great number of men.

The Jews of Thessalonica, however, caught wind of what was happening in Beroea; they traveled there and began to stir up the crowd. In order to avoid any new disturbance, the brethren put Paul on board a ship that was departing for Athens, leaving Silas and Timothy to pursue Christ's work in the city.

The port where he embarked was probably Dium, located 17 miles from Beroea. The crossing to Athens was a voyage of about 248 miles, which took four or five days. Paul and his companions, skirting the coast, had plenty of leisure time to pray and contemplate the historic mountains of Olympus, Ossa, and Pelion. The air was resonant; the sea, violet; a faint pink tinged the mountains; nature smiled, charmed by the sounds of the great lyre of Apollo. But Paul listened to other sounds, another kind of music, the psalmody that Saint John would later call "the song of the Lamb" (Rev 15:3), which is all-encompassing. He was one of those men of God who support their activity by an intense mystical life.

At the entrance to the Strait of Euboea his companions could see Thermopyles, a famous place where Leonidas, leading a thousand Greeks, kept at bay for a while the invasion of Xerxes' armies in 480 B.C. In that place also, Brennus and his Gauls carved out a passage for themselves, settling finally on the high plateaus of Anatolia. Not far from there, on the plain of Marathon, Miltiades covered himself with glory while fighting the Persians in 490 B.C.

A little before reaching Cape Sunium, they could make out, to the right, the silver mines of Laurium, the working of which allowed Themistocles to build up the Athenian navy. Doubling around that very dangerous promontory, which lifted high the crown of the white columns of its temple to Athena, the pilot steered for the Bay of Aegina, where Themistocles defeated the Persian fleet on September 20, 480 B.C., in one of the most glorious naval battles of all times.

The voyage ended at Piraeus, the port of Athens. After passing the Long Walls that had been destroyed by Sylla, Paul's friends left him in good hands and returned to Beroea with Paul's instruction for Silas and Timothy to join him again as soon as possible.

7

The Second Missionary Journey II:
Athens and Corinth

Athens

Like any Hellenized Jew, Paul, who was erudite, pious, zealous, and a rabbi to boot, had received a classical education also, although he did not attain the rank of rhetorician. His letters show an excellent mastery of the Greek language, which cannot be acquired late in life; all critical scholars agree on that. His arrival in Athens, which for centuries had been the center of Hellenism, must have filled him with a strange emotion. The city was still in almost all its original beauty, whereas it appears to us today only as a grandiose ruin, deprived of its marble facings, its broken statues, and its obliterated paintings. How could a Christian help being intimidated and also offended by all those pagan temples and altars, the majestic monuments, and statues of gods, goddesses, and great men?

We will accompany him with Pausanias as our guide, who wrote his *Periēgēsis tēs Hellados*, or "Description of Greece", a hundred years after Paul, and discover what the latter might have admired and criticized in that year, A.D. 50.

Before entering the city by the Gate of Piraeus, Paul could see the building where the citizens stored the costumes used for the yearly procession in honor of Athena.

Close by stood the equestrian statue of Poseidon, brandishing his trident, as well as a temple dedicated to Demeter, the Greek name for the goddess Ceres, containing statues carved by Praxiteles. Making his way into the city, he faced the temple of Dionysius (Bacchus), which was surrounded by many statues dedicated to the gods, which must not have pleased him. Then he found himself on a long street adorned by a magnificent colonnade; under the porticos there were booths that drew plenty of customers.

Paul continued his walk and noticed, on the right, the Pnyx, where Demosthenes pronounced his famous Philippics, in which he appealed, in vain, to the wavering patriotism of his fellow citizens and asked them to resist and to conquer Philip, the king of Macedonia. At the end of the street loomed the triumphal arch celebrating the victory of the Athenians over the cavalry of Cassander along with a magnificent bronze representing Hermes Agoraeos. On the left he discovered the imposing Ceramicus, containing the tombs of famous Athenians. Further on he noticed the Theseum, built in 500 B.C. and still standing today. Beyond the Gate of Dipylum began the Sacred Way to Eleusis.

Now Paul approached the *Stoa Poikilè*, the "Pecilian Portico", a public establishment where Zeno, in the second half of the second century B.C., founded his "Stoic" school, teaching an austere philosophy that insisted on the need for virtue (moral and intellectual excellence) and yet tolerated suicide. Zeno and Cleanthes, Cato and Seneca—Stoics all—ended their days by suicide. Not far from there he could find the garden where Epicurus founded "the school of the garden". Despite his carefree disciples, Epicurus is not what many people think. Philosophers do not regard his teaching as the doctrine of voluptuousness. If it preaches "pleasure", it is only for lack of a term that is less subject to confusion. Pleasure, in the mind of the old

Greek sage, is nothing but the absence of pain, anxiety, and fear. It presupposes a disdain for luxury, the renunciation of all covetousness. It is concerned neither with honors nor with glory nor with action and not even with poetry. The pleasure of Epicurus, you see, had nothing Sybaritic about it, and only by an outright misuse of his words did his supposed disciples in Rome and elsewhere embellish his philosophy with their own indolence and their love of luxury.

When King Oedipus visits Athens, Sophocles, in a charming chorus, has a nightingale sing his praises on the wooded banks of the impetuous Cephisus River. In that olive grove Plato founded his philosophical school, known as the Academy, teaching his disciples the art of interpreting and understanding the visible and the invisible world. His work is for all ages.

Paul kept on discovering in the treasures of Athens the whole history of Greek civilization. There he stood in front of a portico with four columns in the Doric style erected by Caesar Augustus in honor of Athena Archegete, or Athena, the foundress of the city of Athens. Nearby he noted the Tower of the Clock or the Temple of the Winds, built by Andronicus Cyrrhestes, where Socrates (whom the oracle called "the wisest of men") taught his art of living to the young Athenians.

Farther to the east, at the foot of Mount Lycabettus, on the banks of the languid waters of the Ilissus, a river as winding as the Meander in Caria of Anatolia, was located the Lyceum, so called for the sacred wood and the statue of Apollo Lycicus; in that vicinity another disciple of Socrates, Aristotle the Stagirite, tutor of Alexander the Great, had his school. It consisted of a building where Aristotle and his disciples had the custom of walking back and forth, *peripatétikos*, during the course of his presentations.

Somewhat fatigued by the walk, Paul suddenly found himself at a turn in the road facing an enormous out-cropping of rock. At its summit, the highest in the city, loomed the Acropolis—the center of Athens, of Attica, of Greece, and of the world, as the patriot Aristides used to say. Sixty steps led Paul up to the Propylaea [a monumental roofed gateway], built at the time of Pericles. On the right he discovered the winged statue of Victory that recalls Salamis, Marathon, and the great days of Athenian supremacy. A few steps farther on he spied the Erechtaeum, within whose walls one finds the statue of the virgin Polios Athena, guardian of the city, as well as the olive tree that grew from the rock by the intervention of the goddess.

Finally, there was the Parthenon, that architectural jewel, with its gold and ivory statue of Athena sculpted by the great Phidias, showing the goddess springing completely armed from the head of Jupiter. Between the two temples, which cost an immense fortune, stands a third statue, that of Athena *Promachè*, or Athena the warrior, made from the bronze spoils of war taken in the battle of Marathon. It is a statue of gigantic proportions that looms well above the buildings of the Acropolis; its golden helmet and lance, gleaming in the sunlight, caught the eye of every traveler who rounded Cape Sunium.

Farther to the north, a ridge thirty-three feet high and around a quarter of a mile in length extended to the west in the plain. Steps sculpted into the rock led up to the summit of that hill, Ares, the place where the Areopagus gathered, with its three benches roughly hollowed out in a half circle where the judges sat to decide on matters human and divine and to administer justice. Two opposing craggy blocks were reserved for the prosecution and the defense. The tribunal held its sessions in the twilight, which hid the faces of the judges and the advocates so as to allow the magistrates to judge cases without emotion or passion. But in that city, legend never ceases to assert its claims: the deep fissure that one discovers at the base of the rock of the Areopagus is said to be the den of the Erinyes, the vengeful Furies.

The agora [or marketplace] was the center of political and social life in the city; more than three hundred societies met there for discussions or conversation. The main question was always "What's new?" Demosthenes had posed this question to his fellow citizens: "Tell me, is that the only thing you are interested in: walking back and forth on the Agora and asking, 'Is there any news'?" Demades satirically suggested that a big tongue should be featured on the city's coat of arms. Aristophanes described the Athenians as loiterers.

Paul felt a bit lost in the middle of that city populated by temples and statues of all sorts: temples to Apollo, Mars, Vulcan, Aphrodite, the Mother of the Gods, the Twelve Gods, and many others; statues of Hercules and Theseus, of Lycurgus and Solon, of Conon, Pindar, Demosthenes, and the Cretan Epimenides, whom he cites in his Letter to Titus, and...and...he cannot believe his eyes: a statue of the Jewish high priest Hyrcanus, and another of Berenice, the beautiful Jewish princess, before which he would soon appear loaded down with chains. At the beginning of his *Georgics*, after amicably paying homage to Maecenas, his friend, Virgil invokes the tutelary divinities of gardens, forests, stubble-fields, and tilled lands; he salutes Minerva, Pan, Silvanus, the Fauns, and the Dryads. Pliny relates that in his time there were more than two thousand public statues in Athens and innumerable images of the gods in private houses. Every entryway, every gate, every corner had its god to protect it. Petronius sneers, "In Athens it is easier to meet a god than a man." Saint Augustine, not without a certain irony, lists a great number of them in books 4 and 7 of *The City of God*.

Paul, however, did not come there as a tourist. At the first opportunity, as was his custom, he went to the synagogue to meet the children of Israel and those who "feared God". He then saw them again each day at the agora with the other inhabitants of the city. When certain Stoics and Epicurians heard about him, they approached (Acts 17:18, trans. by author), studiously blasé and barely stifling a yawn, and said to one another, "What does this 'seed-picker' [Greek *spermológos*, Latin *seminiverbius*] this story-teller, this babbler want?" Others opined, "He seems to be preaching foreign gods", for they had heard Paul speaking about Jesus and his Resurrection. They asked him to accompany them and made him climb the sixteen steps of the Areopagus leading to the tribunal. There Anaxagoras, Diagoras, Protagoras, and Socrates had been condemned for having proclaimed strange gods.

No doubt somewhat nervous and upset at the outset, Paul turned to his listeners and broached his subject as all the great Athenian orators did: "Men of Athens," and tried to gain the sympathy of his audience with a compliment, a *captatio benevolentiae*, "I perceive that in every way you are very religious. For as I passed along, and observed the objects of your worship, I found also an altar with this inscription, 'To an unknown god'" (Acts 17:22–23). *Agnostōi Theōi*.

This introduction led Paul quite naturally to his subject.

1. God the Creator.

"The God who made the world and everything in it". Here Paul is contradicting the Epicureans, who believed that the world was merely the accidental result of a collision of atoms. He continues: ". . . being Lord of heaven and earth, does not live in shrines made by man, nor is he served by human hands, as though he needed anything, since he himself gives to all men life and breath and everything" (Acts 17:24–25).

Even the Epicureans acknowledged that the God of all things had no need of human beings (see Lucretius II, 650). Euripides, in his play *Hercules Furens*, says, "God, if he is really God, has need of nothing." Lactantius, a fourth-century Christian apologist, cites Seneca: "Temples should not be built for God out of stones piled high; he should be hallowed in the heart of every human being."

2. Concerning man.

"And he made from one [man] every nation of men to live on all the face of the earth, having determined allotted periods and the boundaries of their habitation" (17:26).

Here Paul is twitting the arrogance of the Athenians, who considered themselves superior to all other nations, all those barbarians with their strange languages.

He continues by saying that God partitioned the earth into nations "that they should seek God, in the hope that they might feel after him and find him. Yet he is not far from each one of us, for 'In him we live and move and have our being'; as even some of your poets have said, 'For we are indeed his offspring'" (17:27–28). The latter statement is quoted from *Minos*, by Euripides of Crete.

"Being then God's offspring, we ought not to think that the Deity is like gold, or silver, or stone, a representation by the art and imagination of man" (17:29). In speaking these words, Paul surveyed the panoply of gods and goddesses that surrounded the assembly.

3. He will judge the whole world.

"The times of ignorance God overlooked, but now he commands all men everywhere to repent, because he has fixed a day on which he will judge the world in righteousness by a man whom he has appointed, and of this he has given assurance to all men by raising him from the dead" (17:30–31).

Now when they heard Paul talking about the resurrection of the dead, some of them ridiculed him, while others declared, "We will hear you again about this" (17:32). Paul could not explain the great truths to them nor stir up in them the nobler sentiments that vex weary souls and trouble decadent, corrupt eras. These learned and shrewd Athenians turned away from Paul and from the gospel of the Lord. Several years later, however, they hastened to erect a statue in honor of the emperor Nero with the inscription:

> The Council of the Areopagus and the Council
> of the Six Hundred
> And the people of Athens
> To the Emperor
> The great Nero Caesar Claudius Augustus Germanicus
> Son of God.

Not Christ but Nero?! They are mad, these Athenians! Paul would not fail to point this out later on, in his Letter to the Romans: "Claiming to be wise, they became fools" (1:22). All was not lost, however. "Some men joined him and believed, among them Dionysius the Areopagite and a woman named Damaris and others with them" (Acts 17:34).

A Church in Athens was created after all. Dionysius the Areopagite was the first bishop of Athens, according to another Dionysius who was bishop of Corinth around A.D. 150.

When the emperor Hadrian visited Athens in the year 125, Quadratus and Aristide presented to him two of the most ancient apologies in defense of Christianity. At the Council of Nicaea in 325 the diocese was represented by the bishop and two theologians. The two great saints Basil and Gregory of Nazianzus, as we mentioned, were educated in the pagan schools of the city. Gregory had a fellow student by the name of Julian, who subsequently became emperor and is known to us as Julian the Apostate.

The emperor Justinian closed the schools of philosophy in 529. Seven Sophists still remained, who took up their books and scrolls and left for Persia. The Theseum was transformed into a church dedicated to Saint George of Cappadocia. The Pantheon, the temple of the goddess who fell from the sky, became a Christian temple consecrated to the Mother of God.

A Survey of the Pauline Letters

The period that followed Paul's visit to Athens was extremely busy, especially in the area of correspondence with the various churches that he had founded. Before discussing these letters one by one, it seems appropriate to give a preliminary overview of them.

The order in which Paul's letters appear in our Bibles is not chronological; instead it goes from the longest to the shortest, starting with the ones addressed to communities, followed by the ones sent to individuals.

The only way to reconstruct the order of these letters is by relating them to the facts as they are reported in Acts. Starting from there, the first letters are 1 and 2 Thessalonians, written from Corinth around the year A.D. 51. Of the letters that have come down to us, the next ones are 1 Corinthians, written from Ephesus in around 56 or 57, Galatians around 56, 2 Corinthians, probably from Macedonia (see 2 Cor 2:12) during the autumn of 57; and Romans, several months later in the spring of 58.

The dates that we should assign to Philippians, Philemon, Colossians, and Ephesians depend on the place from which Paul, then a prisoner, wrote them. Tradition claims that all four were written from Rome. Some have objected that the prison from which Paul wrote was not necessarily located in Rome, since Paul was incarcerated on several occasions. Second Corinthians 11:23 suggests and some scholars maintain that Paul spent time also in a jail in Ephesus. We leave to the exegetes the trouble of sorting out the question; meanwhile we will go along with the tradition.

The letters are occasional writings that were surely sent, from the very start, with the purpose of providing Christian instruction. Paul writes not as a man of letters but as a missionary; his letters serve as a substitute for his preaching. Nor did he compose them as we write a letter: he *dictated* them, and they were pronounced viva voce by him. Hence the pacing and harmony of these letters. And so they must likewise be read and judged as exhortations to the people of God. He should therefore be considered as an orator rather than as a writer, but an orator after the example of the prophets, quite naturally endowed with a rhetoric of the heart. With Paul an expression springs from the soul like a swift stream, following a perfectly natural rhythm; nevertheless he knows how to paint a picture with an original and almost brutal force; he can also use the artistic resources of Greek prose as well as the parallelism of the Prophets and Hebrew poetry.

In the great passages in his letters, when the subject inspires and transports him, Paul is truly a poet. Sometimes these passages are not printed as poetic verses in our Bibles, and that is a significant mistake. Examples are the triumphant song about the assurance of salvation (see Rom 8:35–39), the description of the apostle's difficulties (see 1 Cor 5:9–13), his reward (see 2 Tim 2:11–13), the justification for his apostolic work (see 2 Cor 11:21–29), the price of heavenly wisdom (see 1 Cor 2:6–16), his thanksgiving to Christ (see Eph 1:3–14), the poem about Christ's humiliations and exaltations (see Phil 2:6–11), and above all the ardent canticle about charity (see 1 Cor 13:1—14:1). These passages therefore will be cited when the occasion presents itself later in this book.

Corinth

From Athens, where he did not stay for long, Paul traveled to Corinth. *By sea?* In this case a rapid crossing would have brought him to Cenchreae, the eastern port where a statue of Poseidon stood, brandishing his trident and a fish. From there it was only eight miles by foot to arrive at the very center of the city. *By land?* If so, Paul left Athens by the Gate of Dipylon, took the Sacred Way leading to Eleusis, famous for its Mysteries, which were so sacred that Nero himself did not dare to sully them with his presence. At Schoinos was located the Diolkos, or "Bridge Between the Seas", a sort of wooden railroad on which ships of light tonnage were drawn across the Isthmus of Corinth. This allowed mariners to avoid the long and dangerous detour via Cape Matapan. It used to be said, with gallows humor, that a sailor had better make his last will and testament before venturing out into that implacable sea. As early as 600 B.C. engineers had studied the possibility of digging a canal; Alexander the Great and Julius Caesar financed projects to open up a waterway. Nero ordered the work to begin, but it was quickly interrupted. Vespasian brought six thousand Jews from Palestine to resume the work there, but in vain. The canal was not finished until 1893.

In a remote spot deep within a thick pine forest stood the shrine of Poseidon, where every third year the Isthmian Games were celebrated, for which the magistrates of Corinth were responsible, as Horace and Ovid report. The participants had to train and follow a dietary regimen for ten months. Thirty days before the opening of the Games, in the presence of the high priest of the sacrifices, the athletes had to take an oath that they were pure-blooded Greeks, innocent of any crime or act of irreverence. All Greece traveled there to attend the different spectacles. The winner received a crown of laurel or pine branches. "Every athlete exercises self-control in all things. They do it to receive a perishable wreath, but we an imperishable" (1 Cor 9:25).

Jason, aboard his ship the Argos, departed from Corinth on his quest for the Golden Fleece. He abandoned his wife Medea to marry Glaukè, the daughter of King Dreon of Corinth. In revenge Medea killed their children, and Jason's life ended in the most somber tragedy of all Greek mythology. In Corinth also Tantalus made off with a treasure, sure that he would be able to enjoy it in peace. He was punished for it. How? He had to stand in a lake, and every time he bent over to drink from it, the waters receded from his lips. Delicious fruits hung nearby, but when he stretched out his hand to gather one, the branches moved out of reach. Sisyphus attacked the merchants; from his citadel he rolled huge stones to block their road. His punishment? He had to push an enormous round stone to the top of a hill. When he was about to reach the summit, the stone would roll down the slope, and he had to begin all over. Again and again and again for all eternity.

We find this mythology amusing with its fabulous figures, its gods who resemble us so much, its poetic allegories, and its picturesque symbols for natural forces and phenomena. For us it has lost its mystery, its frightening character, and we find these disarmed monsters entertaining. But in ancient times, they instilled fear, with their horrible despotism, their endless wickedness, and their cruelty and injustice; the very uncertainty of the teachings about the nature of the underworld and of the next life inculcated the fear of infinite torments without being offset by the hope of any merited reward.

To illustrate further this sense of terror that was experienced then, it suffices for us to cite just one example, the Erinyes, who by antiphrasis were called the Eumenides, "gracious goddesses".

The faces of these Erinyes were black; their clothing was black; they were not winged; serpents were entangled in their hair and with their arms; their breath poisoned the foam that spewed from their mouths, causing droughts and epidemics.

Any curse uttered by a man awoke them, or rather created a new Erinye who set out in pursuit of the accursed being and drove him to his ruin. Woe to him who, heeding only his anger, utters a curse against his own offspring! Amyntor, the father of Phoenix, and Oedipus cursed their children, and the Erinye, thus awakened, went on to destroy the descendents of those heroes...

But let us return to Corinth. That is where they built the first triremes, or battleships, with three banks of oars, one above the other. Pindar has nothing but praise for Callimachus, who designed the Corinthian style of architecture by contemplating a thistle. Corinth was the first city to organize bullfights and gladiator games. We should also add that the whole Greco-Roman world savored the raisins from Corinth.

In 146 B.C. "Corinth the blessèd", celebrated in song by Homer and Pindar, described by Thucydides and Livy as the light and glory of Greece, was pillaged and destroyed at the order of the Roman consul Lucius Mummius, who carried off to Rome all the treasures of the city, including the bronzes. Corinthian bronze was famous throughout the ancient world, and the "Magnificent Gate" of the Temple in Jerusalem was made of that metal.

For a hundred years the city lay in ruins. Julius Caesar, quite aware of its beauty and strategic position, rebuilt the city 2.5 miles to the north in 47 B.C. and made it a Roman colony. He dubbed it "Colonia Laus Julia Corinthus" in honor of Venus, of whom he considered himself to be a descendent. Holding a key position in the Peloponnisos, equipped with a solid fortress and a center of bustling commerce, Nea Korinthos was very quickly reborn from its ashes. South of the city, Acrocorinthus rose so high that it took more than an hour of difficult climbing to reach the summit by a heavily guarded path.

From there, looking to the east, one could see Athens fifty-three miles away. Apollonius dedicated Acrocorinthus to Aphrodite, whose temple—renowned throughout the ancient world—crowned the summit, which was protected by imposing walls, four hundred soldiers, and fifty of the most ferocious dogs. Officiating at the temple were a thousand priestesses, who were ready to cater to the basest instincts of the visitors under the guise of religion. During the public festivals, the prayers of the sacred prostitutes were considered to be especially effective. These prayers were credited with protecting Corinth during the invasion of Xerxes, and on that occasion Simonides composed an epigram singing their praises.

Beneath the cypress trees of the necropolis outside the city walls was the tomb of Lais, the most famous courtesan from Corinth, who ruined more than one rich citizen with the high price of her charms. She was one of those women who set fire to men and left nothing but ashes. The tomb? It consisted of a marble lioness clutching a sheep in her claws. For the Corinthians this monument was truly the symbol of the terrible power of unbridled sensuality and of the madness of man enslaved by his urges.

At the city gates one could admire the statue of Diogenes, who had walked up and down the streets of the
city in the middle of the day, his lantern lit, looking for
an honest man. Alexander the Great came to pay him
a visit while he was basking in the sun at the entrance
of his barrel. "Can I do something for you?" Alexander
asked him. "Yes, get out of my sunlight", was his response.
Impressed, Alexander retorted, "If I were not Alexander, I
would like to be Diogenes." From the coast, the road led
straight into the center of the city, to the agora, where all
the commercial transactions were carried out at the feet
of the Venus of Cyprus, Thea Kupris, so called by the
red-capped sailors.

Paul found shelter in the house of a Jew named Aquila,
who had been born in the province of Pontus, on the Black
Sea, and had recently arrived from Italy with his wife, Priscilla, following a decree by the emperor Claudius expelling
all the Jews from Rome. This took place in the year 49, as
Orosius reports. The misfortune of the married couple was
also their good fortune, because it enabled them to meet
Paul. Aquila and Priscilla (or Prisca) did not fail to speak
to him at length about the Eternal City, and later on Paul
would say, "I must also see Rome" (Acts 19:21). These two
new disciples were of considerable help to Paul. "Greet
Prisca and Aquila, my fellow workers in Christ Jesus, who
risked their necks for my life, to whom not only I but also
all the churches of the Gentiles give thanks" (Rom 16:3–4;
see 2 Tim 4:19).

Since Aquila plied the same trade, it was quite natural for Paul to stay at his house. The latter made tents
part time to cover his expenses, but his main activity was
proclaiming the Word of God, the good news. "[Paul]
argued in the synagogue every sabbath, and persuaded Jews
and Greeks" (Acts 18:4). Silas and Timothy came from

Macedonia bringing a gift from the Philippians, for which Paul was very grateful (2 Cor 11:9; Phil 4:15). Meanwhile Paul declared to the Jews that Jesus was the Messiah; as a result some of them mounted a violent opposition. Then Paul shook his garments, a symbolic gesture, meant not as a curse but to warn his adversaries to flee the impending crisis. "Your blood be upon your heads! I am innocent. From now on I will go to the Gentiles" (Acts 18:6).

Paul then went to stay with a "God-fearing" man by the name of Titus Justus who had a house next door to the synagogue. Crispus, the ruler of the synagogue, came to believe in the Lord also, with his whole family. Many Corinthians followed his example and were baptized (see Acts 18:8). Then one night, in a vision, the Lord said to Paul, "Do not be afraid, but speak and do not be silent; for I am with you" (18:9–10). Encouraged by this, Paul remained almost two years in Corinth, from the autumn of the year 50 to July of 52, "teaching the word of God among them" (18:11).

Paul's listeners were Jews, Romans, Greeks, "Asiatics" (from the Roman province of Asia); they included masters and slaves, men and women, rich and poor, the unschooled and the learned. The pagans had their magnificent temples; the Jews, their sumptuous synagogues; but the Christians were content to rent a room. They gathered there on the first day of the week in the midst of the hubbub of a very busy city. The Jews attended the service with their heads covered, the Greeks with their heads bare, while the women were veiled. Some were well dressed and well fed; others were hungry and destitute. To that incongruous assembly Paul preached Christ crucified, "a stumbling block to Jews and folly to Gentiles, but to those who are called, both Jews and Greeks, Christ the power of God and the wisdom of God" (1 Cor 1:23–24).

Was Paul a good orator? He was certainly not a rhetorician trained to give the public what they wanted to
hear. These people liked to listen to wordy speeches and
admired them if they lasted for hours, with their long
exordiums, their far-fetched preparations, the interminable
train of their arguments, and their sonorous cadences. Paul
was not that sort of speaker, but it is certain that he had a
gift for controversy and had been trained as a rabbi to be
a very good man of the Law. He himself said, "My speech
and my message were not in plausible words of [human]
wisdom, but in demonstration of the Spirit and of power"
(1 Cor 2:4).

A Church of the Lord in the city of Corinth! The ruler
of the synagogue, as we saw, converted with his whole
household. Many Corinthians accepted the Word of God
and were baptized. Stephanas and his family devoted themselves to the service of the saints (see 1 Cor 16:15–16). Gaius
also converted and would be Paul's host during his second
stay in Corinth. Erastus, the treasurer of the city, and Ter-
tius, to whom Paul dictated the Letter to the Romans,
became Christians, as well as Quartus, Fortunatus, and
Achaicus. And we must not forget Chloe, who headed an
important house, and Phoebe, who would bring the Letter
to the Romans to Rome.

Paul himself describes for us the young Church of
Corinth: "Not many of you were wise according to the
flesh, not many were powerful, not many were of noble
birth; but God chose what is foolish in the world to shame
the wise, God chose what is weak in the world to shame the
strong, God chose what is low and despised in the world,
even things that are not, to bring to nothing things that
are" (1 Cor 1:26–28).

Paul's success did not fail to arouse the hostility of a
group of Jews in the city. They brought Paul before the

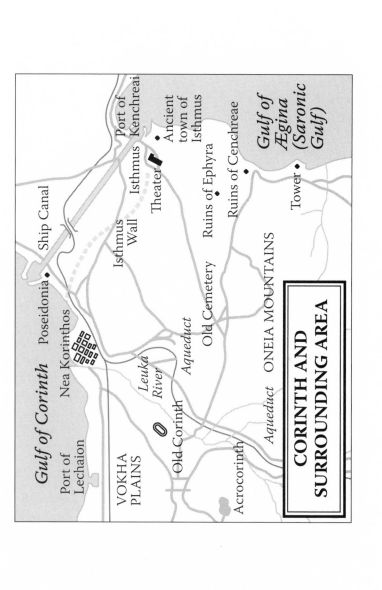

CORINTH AND SURROUNDING AREA

Gulf of Corinth

Port of Lechaion

VOKHA PLAINS

Poseidonia •

Nea Korinthos

Ship Canal

Port of Kenchreai

Port of Isthmus

Isthmus Wall

Theater

Ancient town of Isthmus

Ruins of Ephyra

Ruins of Cenchreae

Gulf of Ægina (Saronic Gulf)

Tower •

Leuka River

Aqueduct

Old Cemetery

Old Corinth

Acrocorinth

Aqueduct

Aqueduct

ONEIA MOUNTAINS

tribunal to be judged by Gallio, the new proconsul, declaring, "This man is persuading men to worship God contrary to the law" (Acts 18:13). Paul was about to respond when Gallio retorted, "If it were a matter of wrongdoing or vicious crime, I should have reason to bear with you,... but since it is a matter of questions about words and names and your own law, see to it yourselves; I refuse to be a judge of these things" (18:14–15). And he sent them away from the tribunal. The exasperated Jews then seized Sosthenes, the ruler of the synagogue, no doubt the successor to Crispus, and beat him unmercifully in the presence of the proconsul. But Gallio did not take the trouble to react.

Who was this Gallio, the one who saved Paul in Corinth? Marcus Annaeus took the name of Gallio when he was adopted by the rhetor Lucius Junius Gallio; he was the brother of the famous philosopher Seneca, who dedicated to him his works "On anger" and "On the happy life", and speaks of him in laudatory terms: "No one is kinder to his closest friends than Gallio is to the rest of humanity."

Gallio arrived in Corinth as proconsul of the province of Achaia in 51 or 52, according to an inscription discovered at Delphi. A proconsul appointed for one year was responsible for all administrative, judiciary, and military matters in his province and was assisted by legates such as the quaestor for finances, or "paymaster". His administration was supported by a direct tax, the stipendium. This tax was collected by the publicans, who were organized under a general director in Rome and provincial directors. The local communities responsible for collecting taxes depended on local banks or paid moneylenders, *negotiatores*, who lent at compound interest ranging 8%–12%, sometimes at a much higher rate.

Yes, what a contrast between the glorious Gallio and the poor Jewish preacher Paul! And yet countless individuals would never have heard about the proconsul except for that brief encounter with the apostle. Like a speck of dust, he is visible only in the bright sunlight of faith!

Paul left Corinth and traveled to the port of Cenchreae, where Phoebe welcomed him with such hospitality that he never forgot it (see Rom 16:1). Here too Paul had his head shaved "for he had [taken] a vow" (Acts 18:18). Every Jew could take a Nazirite vow of thanksgiving for a favor obtained, for having escaped from grave danger or from a serious illness. The one who made this vow became a nazir during the entire time of his vow, usually thirty days. During that period he had to abstain from wine and shave his head. If at the end of those thirty days the Nazirite was not in Jerusalem, he had to preserve the locks of hair until his next visit to the city, purify himself for seven days, shave his head again, and burn all the locks thus accumulated in the fire for the sacrifices (see Num 6:13–21).

From Cenchreae Paul set sail for Ephesus, on the west coast of Anatolia, where, accompanied by Aquila and Priscilla, he would surely be able to find work. Ephesus, indeed, was renowned for the quality of its tents. Alcibiades considered himself unsatisfied unless he obtained a tent made in that city. But for Paul, Ephesus was just a port of call. As was his custom, he took the opportunity to go to the synagogue to proclaim the Word of the Lord. He was well received and his listeners asked him to remain with them for a time. He could not oblige and left them, saying, "I will return to you [*tou theou thelontos*], if God wills" (Acts 18:21). And he boarded a ship for Caesarea Maritima, no doubt in late summer of the year 52. From there he traveled to Jerusalem, greeted the brethren, bid adieu to Silas and, still accompanied by Timothy, returned to Antioch.

Thus ended his second missionary journey.

Meanwhile in Ephesus, which Paul had just left, a Jew arrived by the name of Apollos, a native of Alexandria in Egypt, the fatherland of Philo, the famous Neoplatonic philosopher and great exegete of the Old Testament. Apollos was an excellent orator, well versed in the Scriptures, and well instructed in the ways of the Lord. Full of fervor, "he spoke and taught accurately the things concerning Jesus, though he knew only the baptism of John. He began to speak boldly in the synagogue" (Acts 18:25–26). When Aquila and Priscilla heard him, they took him home with them and explained to him the more perfect way of the Lord. With great humility, Apollos accepted the lessons given by these simple people and acquired a better understanding of the gospel of Christ.

When Apollos announced his intention to go to Achaia, the brethren recommended him to the disciples of Corinth. He confirmed the Corinthians in their faith, converting the Jews and showing by the Scriptures that Jesus was the Messiah. "I planted, Apollos watered, but God gave the growth" (1 Cor 3:6).

The Two Letters to the Thessalonians

During his stay in Corinth, Paul had not been able to visit his converts in Thessalonica, and he was concerned about their progress in the faith. Timothy had been sent to them during Paul's stay in Athens and was able to report that the brethren were still faithful, despite the persecution, and wanted to see Paul among them again.

Many of those brethren were desolate because some among them had died without having experienced the return of Christ. Others used this expectant waiting as an excuse for doing nothing and living a disorderly life, and still others abused their spiritual graces.

These two letters were addressed by Paul, Silvanus, and Timothy to the second of the churches founded by Paul in Macedonia after he had crossed the sea at Troas during his second missionary journey.

In 1 Thessalonians 1:9–10, Paul reminds his dear Thessalonians about their conversion, "how you turned to God from idols, to serve a living and true God, and to wait for his Son from heaven, whom he raised from the dead, Jesus who delivers us from the wrath to come." This is an occasional letter and not a doctrinal treatise, and yet it sums up for us almost the entire contents of the Christian religion in its freshness, purity, and beauty, penned by a contemporary of Christ, around twenty years after the Crucifixion.

The community seems to have been made up largely of Gentiles, because Paul says to its members that they have suffered, from their countrymen, the same persecution that the churches of Judea underwent at the hands of the Jews (see 2:14). He deems it necessary to remind them to avoid debauchery and to marry instead (see 4:3–8); they should not be lazy—far from it!—but should work (see 4:9–12). They have no reason to worry about the fate of believers who die, for when the Lord descends from heaven, the living and the dead shall rise together to meet him in the air "and so we shall always be with the Lord" (4:17; see 4:13–16, 18). The hour of his coming cannot be predicted with certainty, but it will come (see 5:1–11).

"May the God of peace himself sanctify you wholly; and may your spirit and soul and body be kept sound and blameless at the coming of our Lord Jesus Christ" (5:23).

From all this emerges the central idea of First Thessalonians: the faithful must trust Paul when he preaches to them the imminent coming of the Lord. The Thessalonians were waiting for the return of Jesus, who delivers us from the wrath to come, and not all of them paid sufficient attention

to the problem of their sanctification in the here and now
(see 3:13; 4:12; 4:15; 5:24).

And the letter ends with a simple sentence: "The grace
of our Lord Jesus Christ be with you" (5:28), an expression
that Christians will repeat down through the centuries.

Serious historians such as Tacitus, Suetonius, and Dio
Cassius tell us about marvelous signs, distressing omens,
and unheard-of prodigies throughout the Greco-Roman
empire during the period that we are studying. Some people were even proclaiming the end of the world. These
predictions were echoed in Thessalonica and had sowed
panic among many Christians. The rumors were aggra-
vated by false teachers who wrote letters purportedly from
Paul, and also by an erroneous interpretation of the first
letter that he had addressed to them.

Christian prophets seemed to confirm the pagan augu-
ries, and some of the brethren who were not firm in their
faith were so upset by them that they ceased all useful work
and sank into acedia, which is spiritual sloth or indiffer-
ence. If the Lord is near, what good does it do to apply
yourself? Why tire yourself? They stopped attending to
their ordinary obligations so as to lead a life of idleness,
gazing at the sky and hoping ardently for the return of the
Messiah. And when hunger tormented them, they turned
to the brethren and were fed at their expense.

When he was informed about this situation, Paul decided
to remedy it with a Second Letter to the Thessalonians.

In the first chapter, which is very short, he greets the
brethren and thanks the Lord for their charity, faith, and
patience. In the second, he corrects their false notions about
Judgment Day. Although it is true that that day is near, it is
not necessarily imminent. First the apostasy must develop,
the man of lawlessness must appear, the son of perdition, the
adversary, who will oppose everything that men consider

to be godly (see 2 Thess 2:2–6). This mystery of lawlessness is already at work; it needs only to do away with the
one "who now restrains it". Then "the lawless one will be
revealed, and the Lord Jesus will slay him with the breath
of his mouth and destroy him by his appearing and his
coming" (2:7–8).

In the third chapter Paul exhorts the brethren not to
live in idleness at the expense of others. And he issues the
famous statement "If any one will not work, let him not
eat" (3:10). About himself Paul says, "We worked night
and day, that we might not burden any of you" (3:8). Here
again, the laziness of the Thessalonians seems to come from
their errors concerning eschatology. They have heard,
"either by spirit [i.e., by some inspiration] or by word, or
by letter purporting to be from us, to the effect that the
day of the Lord has come" (2:2). To the brethren who are
walking faithfully and courageously in the way of Christ,
he says, "Do not be weary in well-doing" (3:13).

Paul has stopped dictating. He takes the quill from the
hand of his secretary and, perhaps because of the existence
of those counterfeit epistles, he deems it helpful to conclude
his letter *manu mea*: "I, Paul, write this greeting with my
own hand. This is the mark [or signature] in every letter
of mine; it is the way I write. The grace of our Lord Jesus
Christ be with you all" (3:17–18).

8

The Third Missionary Journey

Ephesus

Minoans came first and after them Trojans, fleeing from fallen Troy. Later came Androcles of Athens, Croesus, Xerxes, Alexander, Hannibal, Julius Caesar, Cleopatra, Saint Paul and, somewhat later Saint John and the Virgin Mary.

They came to Ephesus, on the Cayster (or Kaystros) River with its famous swans. According to Homer, Ephesus was "on the vast plain of Asia". Mountains surrounded the fertile valley except to the west, where the sea, flecked with gold, glittered beneath the slanting rays of the setting sun.

In 1040 B.C., the son of King Codrus, in Athens, founded a Greek colony at that place and was taken to task by armed virgins, the guardians of the original temple. This incident perhaps gave rise to the legend of the Amazons. In 560 B.C. Croesus, king of Lydia, seized the city.

Xenophon and Plutarch relate that the city was supplied by two ports. Lysander built the piers there and an arsenal around the year 400 B.C. Thanks to the larger of the two ports, Panormus, Ephesus became the most opulent city in Asia, as Ovid notes. Pliny calls it "the Light of Asia", and the inscription on the temple of Diana mentioned that it was "the first and most important metropolis of the region of Asia". The city walls built by Lysimachus, a general and friend of Alexander the Great, were 10 feet thick, 2.5 miles long, and fortified by imposing towers; the bulwarks enclosed an urban center covering almost 25 acres. But the city extended well beyond the ramparts.

In 133 B.C., Attalus III, by his last will and testament, ceded his kingdom of Pergamum to the Roman republic, which made it a province of Asia. In 88 B.C., the Ephesians sided with Mithridates of Pontus and massacred the Roman residents. To avenge that insult to the honor of Rome, the dictator Cornelius Sylla sacked the city four years later. In 51 B.C., Cicero visited the city, and in 48 Julius Caesar reorganized the province.

In Ephesus, in 500 B.C., Heraclitus, who originated the concept of the Logos, ridiculed the superstition of the Ephesians. Here, too, the virtuous life of the philosopher Hermodorus served as a permanent rebuke to the city's vices, and so the inhabitants banished him, begging him to practice his virtue elsewhere. He traveled to Rome, where he explained the laws of Solon to the decemviri, which gave rise to the Law of the Twelve Tables and formed the basis of Roman law. As a token of gratitude, the city of Rome erected a statue in his honor.

Again at Ephesus, Hipponax composed iambics so virulent that he was exiled to Clazomenae, on the gulf of Smyrna. Here, too, Apelles, the famous painter, plied his trade, as did Zeuxis, who painted such realistic frescos that even the birds were fooled and came to pick at his bunches of grapes. The shepherd Pixodorus discovered in the vicinity an immense quarry of very fine marble, which Phidias, Praxiteles, Polyclitus, Scopas, Myron, and others used in creating their masterpieces.

The geographer Artemidorus was so bold as to launch into a description of the earth's globe. Another Artemidorus wrote the work entitled *Oneirocritica* (*The Interpretation*

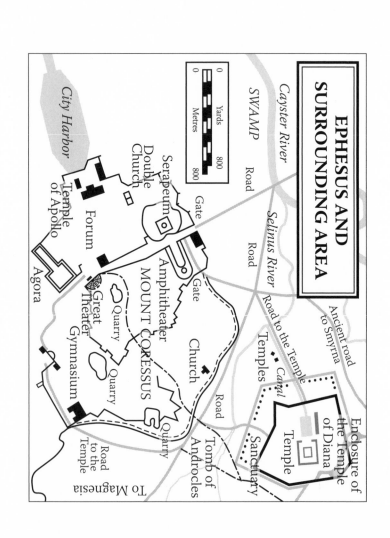

EPHESUS AND SURROUNDING AREA

Cayster River

SWAMP   Road

Selinus River

Road

0   Yards   800
0   Metres   800

City Harbor

Double
Church

Serapeum

Gate

Temple
of Apollo

Forum

Agora

Amphitheater

MOUNT CORESSUS

Great
Theater

Gymnasium

Quarry

Quarry

Quarry

Gate

Church

Road

Road to the Temple

Temples

Canal

Ancient road
to Smyrna

Enclosure of
the Temple
of Diana

Temple

Sanctuary

Tomb of
Androcles

Road
to the
Temple

To Magnesia

of Dreams). A man by the name of Phormion gave courses in military strategy, which Hannibal, the famous Carthaginian general, declared to be sheer idiocy. Much later, Nero employed the services of a citizen of Ephesus, the Jewish astrologer Balbillus, who became his confidant.

A broad, paved promenade 1.25 miles long was flanked on either side by libraries, meeting rooms, and little second-rate temples. It started at the port of Panormus and ended at the largest of all Greek theaters, which reportedly could hold as many as twenty-five thousand people. Farther to the north the pedestrian would find the stadium or circus, which showcased all the sporting events that the Greeks were so fond of: foot races, discus and javelin throwing, wrestling, fighting with wild animals. More often than not the *bestiarii* who fought those animals were men who had been sentenced to death. They confronted the beasts completely naked and succumbed to their claws and fangs. Paul compares those *bestiarii* with the apostles of the gospel: "For I think that God has exhibited us apostles as last of all, like men sentenced to death; because we have become a spectacle to the world, to angels and to men.... What do I gain if, humanly speaking, I fought with beasts at Ephesus?" (1 Cor 4:9; 15:32). These words were written by Paul while he was staying in Ephesus (see 1 Cor 16:8).

The Temple of Diana (Artemis)

The Persians abhorred idols, and when they invaded Anatolia and other regions they set fire to the temples so as to destroy them. But Xerxes spared the temple of Diana, which was also called the Artemision, because of its great beauty. Chersiphon had been its architect in the sixth century B.C. Croesus and other potentates brought exquisite columns and magnificent statues as an offering.

Herostratus was eager for glory; he got it by setting fire to the dome of the Artemision October 13–14 in the year 356 B.C. Hegesias of Magnesia, a renowned satirist, remarked that it was not at all surprising that the temple should burn, given that Artemis was absent on that occasion, quite busy serving as midwife at the birth of Alexander the Great. Plutarch commented that that observation was icy enough to extinguish those flames all by itself.

After his victory over the Persians at the Granicus in 324 B.C., Alexander offered to provide the enormous amount of capital necessary to rebuild the temple on one condition: that it would be named in his honor. The proud Ephesians jealously declined his offer, disguising their refusal with flattery: "It is not fitting for a god to erect a temple to another god." Alexander had to be content with a sacrifice to the goddess.

From each of the four sides, a stairway of fourteen steps led to the courtyard of the temple, which was enormous in size: 328 feet by 151 feet by 59 feet, topped with an immense roof made of cedar. Thirty-six of its columns were sculpted, one of them by Scopas. Eight of these columns were used, much later, in the construction of the Hagia Sophia in Constantinople. The temple was four times as large as the Parthenon but smaller than Notre-Dame Cathedral in Paris (390 feet by 144 feet by 105 feet). It contained the masterpiece of Calliphon of Samos, "Patrocles Putting on the Armor of Achilles", as well as the great fresco of the famous Apelles depicting "Alexander the Great Hurling Thunder", the value of which was estimated at twenty talents, a considerable sum. The walls were covered with votive offerings left by grateful devotees. In the center stood an altar sumptuously decorated by Praxiteles. Behind a richly embroidered curtain of purple was the "Great Diana of the Ephesians", fallen from the sky and venerated by the entire world. Was it made of cedar, olive wood, or ivory? No one knew, Pliny tells us.

The idol was crowned with a tower, its torso was covered with breasts or perhaps with bull testicles, a symbol of generation, and from the waist to the feet she was swathed like a mummy. The whole statue was covered with magical inscriptions called "the Ephesian writings", which were copied out as charms. Around it stood other statues that purportedly shed real tears. All day long the air was freshened by Oriental perfumes. The walls multiplied the spectacle by means of concave mirrors, and fountains projected bursts of light like a dew of diamonds.

At the rear of the temple was the treasure of kings and nations; for the sanctuary was reputedly so inviolable that there was no other place in the world, except for the Temple of Jerusalem, where they could deposit their treasure more securely. Xenophon placed a sum of money there after his anabasis, the long march with his ten thousand Greek soldiers. Later, Aristides describes this place as "the central treasury of all [the province of] Asia". Julius Caesar on two occasions saved the treasure from the rapacious hands of Scipio and Amphius. Nero had no scruples about it: he pillaged all the temples of Greece and Asia Minor, not even sparing the temple of Diana.

The high priest was accompanied by a swarm of priestesses whose lascivious dances incited men to the grossest and most degrading debauchery. The month of May was dedicated to Artemis and great festivals were held then in her honor. The Olympic games that were organized there proved to be as popular as those in Corinth and Olympus. That was the sort of opulent and decadent city to which Paul traveled in A.D. 54 to preach the good news.

Paul in Ephesus

Before arriving in Ephesus, Paul, accompanied by Gaius from Derbe, passed through Galatia to strengthen the recent converts in their faith and to take up a collection for the benefit of the brethren in Jerusalem. Making their way through Phrygia, they followed the course of the Hermus River as far as Sardis and then crossed a chain of mountains to the Cayster Valley, which led to Ephesus.

Paul found there a certain number of believers who had been baptized in the name of John the Baptist.

> And Paul said, "John baptized with the baptism of repentance, telling the people to believe in the one who was to come after him, that is, Jesus." On hearing this, they were baptized in the name of the Lord Jesus. And when Paul had laid his hands upon them, the Holy Spirit came on them; and they spoke with tongues and prophesied. There were about twelve of them in all. (Acts 19:4–7)

Paul then went to the synagogue and over the course of three months spoke there with authority, proclaiming the Word of God and seeking to convince the members of the congregation. Alas! There were hard-hearted, disbelieving men among them who disparaged the New Way among the congregants. Paul then broke off all contact with them and, accompanied by his new disciples, took refuge in the school [or meeting hall] of Tyrannus. He taught there for two years, so that all the inhabitants of Ephesus and the surrounding areas, Jews and Greeks, could hear the good news. Among them, no doubt, was "my beloved Epaenetus, who was the first convert in Asia in Christ" (Rom 16:5).

The Lord worked extraordinary miracles through the agency of Paul; applying linens or handkerchiefs that had touched his body was enough to make sicknesses vanish and to drive out evil spirits. Now some itinerant Jewish

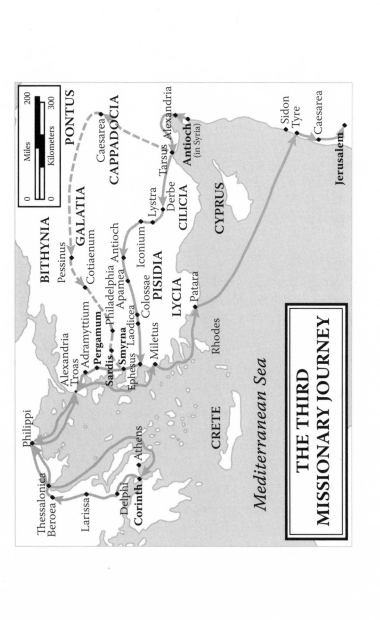

THE THIRD
MISSIONARY JOURNEY

exorcists hit on the idea of making use of the Lord's name also, saying, "I adjure you by the Jesus whom Paul preaches" (Acts 19:13). The seven sons of the high priest Sceva were acting in this way. But the evil spirit they were trying to exorcise answered: "Jesus I know, and Paul I know; but who are you?" (19:15). And the possessed man lunged at them and mistreated them so badly that it was all they could do, naked and bleeding, to escape the house where they had attempted the exorcism. "And this became known to all residents of Ephesus, both Jews and Greeks; and fear fell upon them all; and the name of the Lord Jesus was extolled" (19:17).

Riot in the City

During Paul's stay in Ephesus some big trouble started. An inhabitant of the city by the name of Demetrius, a silversmith by profession, made charms out of silver with the effigy of Diana. He sold them to visitors to the temple, and this was a major source of income for him and the other craftsmen. Troubled by Paul's success, he assembled the silversmiths and other artisans and harangued them as follows:

> Men, you know that from this business we have our wealth. And you see and hear that not only at Ephesus but almost throughout all Asia this Paul has persuaded and turned away a considerable company of people, saying that gods made with hands are not gods. And there is danger not only that this trade of ours may come into disrepute but also that the temple of the great goddess Artemis may count for nothing, and that she may even be deposed from her magnificence, she whom all Asia and the world worship. (Acts 19:25–27)

At these words the assembly, seething with rage, began to shout, "Great is Artemis of the Ephesians!" (19:28). This was the slogan the crowd chanted during processions in honor of Diana (Artemis).

After the meeting, the unrest spread swiftly through the entire city. Unable to find Paul, the crowd seized Gaius and Aristarchus, two Macedonians, and dragged them through a chaotic scene in the streets toward the amphitheater. Paul turned deadly pale: he too wanted to go to the amphitheater; fortunately his disciples opposed his plan. Among his friends were several Asiarchs who told him in no uncertain terms that he must not venture into the center of the city. The Asiarchs were the high priests of the province of Asia who supervised the cult of the emperor and the games. Very wealthy men were chosen for this honor, since they had to cover most of the expenses related to that cult. They were also responsible for the good conduct of the population in the province, and an uncontrolled mob was their worst nightmare.

The crowd continued shouting in a most disorderly fashion. The evangelist Luke remarks, not without irony, that "most of them did not know why they had come together" (Acts 19:32) as a mob. Some individuals in the multitude explained the situation to a certain Alexander, whom the Jews put forward, and the latter, holding up one hand, was about to speak. But when they heard that he was Jewish, they all resumed their chant in unison, which lasted two hours: "Great is Artemis of the Ephesians" (19:34) "*Megálē hē Ártemis Ephesíōn*."

Exhausted by the effort of shouting, the demonstrators finally calmed down, and the *grammateus*, or clerk of the city, was able to make himself heard:

"Men of Ephesus, what man is there who does not know that the city of the Ephesians is temple keeper of the great Artemis, and of the sacred stone that fell from the sky?

Seeing then that these things cannot be contradicted, you ought to be quiet and do nothing rash. For you have brought these men here who are neither sacrilegious nor blasphemers of our goddess. If therefore Demetrius and the craftsmen with him have a complaint against any one, the courts are open, and there are proconsuls; let them bring charges against one another. But if you seek anything further, it shall be settled in the regular assembly. For we are in danger of being charged with rioting today, there being no cause that we can give to justify this commotion." And when he had said this, he dismissed the assembly. (Acts 19:35–40)

Once the uprising had been calmed, Paul rejoined his disciples to encourage them. Then he bid his adieux and departed for Macedonia.

The Two Letters to the Corinthians

During Paul's sojourn in Ephesus, Timothy had returned to Corinth and had written a pessimistic report about the state of the Church in that city. A little later, several members of Chloe's household—Stephanas, Fortunatus, and Archaichus—brought a letter from the community in Corinth asking Paul to clarify certain points of doctrine and of everyday Christian practice. From that letter and from his conversations with the envoys, Paul was able to get a very comprehensive idea of the situation, and it was not encouraging. He had worked for years in that city, but during his long absence since then problems had accumulated.

Paul did not despair. He called back Timothy, who had set out by land, and sent as his replacement Titus with a commission to deal with the most pressing matters. For now he gave up his plans to go to Corinth. He summoned Sosthenes, the synagogue ruler who had converted, and dictated to him the two Letters to the Corinthians. One was written in Ephesus in the spring of the year 57, while the other was probably sent from Macedonia in the autumn of that same year.

In a clear and magnificently nuanced picture, the two letters aptly inform us about the relations, the situation, the dissensions, and the struggles in one of the most important communities in the early Church. Against the background of this *ekklesia* located in a very cosmopolitan city, the communal and pastoral ideal of the apostle, who is consumed with zeal for souls, stands out sharply.

In the first letter, Paul forcefully takes a stand against the immorality that seemed to reign in the community. "It is actually reported that there is immorality among you, and of a kind that is not found even among pagans; for a man is living with his father's wife.... Let him who has done this be removed from among you" (1 Cor 5:1–2).

He opposes even more vehemently their tendency to quarrel and especially the partisan spirit that was tearing the young Church apart. "I say this to your shame. Can it be that there is no man among you wise enough to decide between members of the brotherhood, but brother goes to law against brother, and that before unbelievers?" (6:5–6). He then answers the questions that had been asked him concerning the right attitude of Christians toward marriage and in their relations with the pagan cults. Then he teaches at length about the interior life of faith, community life, the Last Supper, the gifts of grace, and the resurrection of the body.

The thirteenth chapter is not only the climax of this letter, but also the heart of Paul's letters, based on sacred Scripture in its entirety, the most exalted revelation of Christianity in its purest and fullest flowering; it is the canticle of charity, without which all religion is just a sounding brass or a tinkling cymbal, and this virtue is the greatest in the trinity of faith, hope, and charity.

> If I speak in the tongues of men and of angels, but have not love, I am a noisy gong or a clanging cymbal....and if I have all faith, so as to remove mountains, but have not love, I am nothing. If I give away all I have, and if I deliver my body to be burned, but have not love, I gain nothing.
>
> Love is patient and kind; Love is not jealous or boastful; it is not arrogant or rude....Love never ends....For now we see in a mirror dimly, but then face to face. Now I know in part; then I shall understand fully, even as I have been fully understood.
>
> So faith, hope, love abide, these three; but the greatest of these is love. (1 Cor 13:1–5, 8, 12, 13)

In the Second Letter to the Corinthians, Paul lays the blame on agitators, some Jews from outside the community; he clarifies the relations between Judaism and Christianity and successfully refutes the insulting reproaches of his enemies against him personally. Despite his many cares, he finds the time to organize a collection for the brethren in Jerusalem. And so, pressured by his adversaries, he reveals to us the depth of his apostolic soul, burning with love for Jesus. In this letter we have a priceless document that makes known to us the interior life of the great apostle to the Gentiles.

Toward the end of the letter, "like a madman" (2 Cor 11:23), Paul feels compelled to remind his readers about all that he has suffered for the cause of Christ. He explains that he has often been near death.

> Five times I have received at the hands of the Jews the forty lashes less one. Three times I have been beaten with rods; once I was stoned. Three times I have been shipwrecked; a night and a day I have been adrift at sea; on frequent

journeys, in danger from rivers, danger from robbers, danger from my own people, danger from Gentiles, danger in the city, danger in the wilderness, danger at sea, danger from false brethren; in toil and hardship, through many a sleepless night, in hunger and thirst, often without food, in cold and exposure. And, apart from other things, there is the daily pressure upon me of my anxiety for all the churches. (2 Cor 11:24–28)

9

The Ascent to Jerusalem

During his sojourn in Ephesus, no doubt in late A.D. 56, Paul heard reports of another crisis, this time in Galatia, where the Judaizers were sowing trouble. Paul found himself in a difficult situation. He would gladly have gone to visit his dear Galatians, but his missionary activity did not allow it. So he turned once more to his secretary, who began to record the message that we know by the name of the Letter to the Galatians.

The Celts in Galatia

Before summarizing this letter we must discuss briefly the people of Galatia, whom Paul loved so much.

During the fourth century B.C., the Celts had slowly invaded eastern Europe, driving out the inhabitants who had settled there centuries before. Some of those tribes established themselves in the central and northern regions of present-day France. In 390 B.C. they could be found in Italy; they might even have seized Rome had it not been for the cacophonous intervention of the Capitoline geese. Around 300 B.C. the Celts made their way into Greece and were turned back at Delphi. In 275 B.C. more than twenty thousand men, plus women and children, settled in Asia Minor. Forty years later, Attalus I, king of Pergamum, offered them the high plateau in the interior, which they colonized. The capital of one of these Celtic tribes—or Galatians, as they were called in Greek—was Pessinus, center of the cult of Cybele, whose sacred image, fallen from the sky, was sent to Rome to protect the Eternal City from the threat of the terrible Hannibal in 204 B.C.

Midas, the famous Midas, the Phrygian king who turned everything that he touched into gold, while visiting the high plateau of Anatolia, discovered an anchor thrust into the ground. He built a city at that spot which he called Ancyra, Greek for "anchor". It became the chief center of the province of Galatia and is today, under the name of Ankara, the capital of Turkey.

The county seat of the third district of Galatia was Tavium, noted for its sacred wood, perhaps commemorating a Druid past; in antiquity it was dedicated to Zeus with his colossal statue.

Julius Caesar considered the Celts of France and Belgium as peoples that were "very fickle in their plans, eager for novelty and completely unworthy of trust". These traits were found also among the Gallic peoples in the East. One day they were fighting for the king of Pontus, the next day for his enemy, the king of Pergamum. They were mercenaries, soldiers of fortune. Four hundred Galatians, tall in stature with gilded arms and breastplates, made up the bodyguard of Cleopatra VII until the day when, with their customary casualness, they changed sides to serve Herod, her most implacable enemy.

In 25 B.C., Caesar Augustus annexed to the territory of the Galatians part of the province of Pontus to the northeast, a bit of Phrygia to the southwest, and the greater part of Lycaonia to the south. The whole region formed the new Roman province of Galatia. Located in the south of that new entity were the cities of Antioch, Iconium, Lystra, and Derbe. When Paul wrote his letter to the "Galatians" it was probably that southern part that he was addressing.

The Letter to the Galatians

The Judaizers, in their appeals to the Gentiles converted by Paul, maintained that he was not an apostle and that his message did not constitute the true gospel. Certainly they could believe in Christ, but they had to practice circumcision and follow the dietary laws of the Jews.

The situation was very serious. All the freedom of the New Way of Christ had been called into question. Paul was shaken by it to the depths of his soul. In his Letter to the Galatians he summarizes his position. It is a letter dictated in haste, with mangled, incorrect phrases and highly charged with emotion; one senses vividly the passion that inspired him then.

The Apostles of Freedom

"Paul, an apostle—not from men nor through man, but through Jesus Christ and God the Father, who raised him from the dead" (Gal 1:1). No Old Testament prophet ever dared to speak in that manner.

From the outset Paul explodes. Instead of the customary formula of praise or thanksgiving—an omission that does not bode well at all—he expresses his deep disappointment: "I am astonished that you are so quickly deserting him who called you in the grace of Christ and turning to a different gospel" (1:6). And he utters a vehement curse: "Even if we, or an angel from heaven, should preach to you a gospel contrary to that which we preached to you, let him be accursed! [*Anathema esto*]" (1:8). In the next sentence he repeats this curse. Further on Paul reprimands the Galatians for their many faults. He lists no fewer than fifteen.

Paul continues by proving the independence of his authority, based on divine revelation.

> Brethren, I would have you know that the gospel which was preached by me is not man's gospel. For I did not receive it from man, nor was I taught it, but it came through a revelation of Jesus Christ....But when he...was pleased to reveal his Son to me, in order that I might preach him among the Gentiles,...I went away into Arabia; and again I returned to Damascus.
>
> Then after three years I went up to Jerusalem to visit Cephas, and remained with him fifteen days. (1:11–12, 15–18)

The Gospel of Freedom

The Christian experience of the Galatians themselves proves the truth of Paul's gospel. "O foolish Galatians! Who has bewitched you, before whose eyes Jesus Christ was publicly portrayed as crucified?...Does he who supplies the Spirit to you and works miracles among you do so by works of the law, or by hearing with faith?" (Gal 3:1, 5).

History, too, proves the truth of Paul's gospel. Your false Jewish teachers talk a lot about Abraham. Well, then, let's talk about Abraham. How was he justified? "Thus Abraham 'believed God, and it was reckoned to him as righteousness.' So you see that it is men of faith who are the sons of Abraham" (3:6–7).

The Old Testament is another proof of the authenticity of Paul's mission. Certainly, if a man observes the Law perfectly, he will be saved (see Lev 18:5). But can he observe it without fault? For it is written: "Cursed be every one who does not abide by all things written in the book of the law, and do them" (Gal 3:10; see Deut 27:26). But it is obvious that no man can, in God's sight, be justified by the law; for "He who through faith is righteous shall live" (Gal 3:11; see Hab 2:4).

The true nature of Christ's action is an additional proof of the truth of Paul's mission. "Christ redeemed us from the curse of the law, having become a curse for us—for it is written, 'Cursed be every one who hangs on a tree'—that in Christ Jesus the blessing of Abraham might come upon the Gentiles, that we might receive the promise of the Spirit through faith" (Gal 3:13–14).

Life in Freedom

> For freedom Christ has set us free; stand fast therefore, and do not submit again to a yoke of slavery.
>
> Now I, Paul, say to you that if you receive circumcision, Christ will be of no advantage to you.... You are severed from Christ, you who would be justified by the law; you have fallen away from grace.... For in Christ Jesus neither circumcision nor uncircumcision is of any avail, but faith working through love. (Gal 5:1–2, 4, 6)
>
> For you were called to freedom, brethren; only do not use your freedom as an opportunity for the flesh, but through love be servants of one another. For the whole law is fulfilled in one word, "You shall love your neighbor as yourself." (5:13–14)

Paul adds a personal note: "Henceforth let no man trouble me; for I bear on my body the marks of Jesus" (6:17). Just as the priests of the pagan idols were marked with a red-hot iron, Paul bore on his body the scars of the ill treatment that he had endured for Christ. The royal mark, "character regis", was branded on the hand of a Roman soldier to prevent him from deserting, and so too the mark of Christ was imprinted on Paul's body.

The letter ends with a blessing: "The grace of our Lord Jesus Christ be with your spirit, brethren. Amen" (6:18).

The winter of 57–58 was coming to an end. Winter had given Paul much leisure to reflect on a letter that he wanted to send to a community that he did not know but which he ardently desired to visit some day. He had expressed this desire not long before in speaking about a visit to Jerusalem: "I must also see Rome" (Acts 19:21). One day he called his scribe, gathered up the tablets covered with a thin layer of wax as well as the sheets of papyrus, and set about dictating his letter "to all God's beloved in Rome" (Rom 1:7).

Letter to the Romans

This letter is addressed to a community that Paul had never visited, this letter is the longest one that he wrote: around seventy-one hundred words. It therefore amounts to almost one-quarter of the Pauline literature. The most obvious objectives of this missive are: (1) to give a summary of the gospel preached by Paul (see 1:15–17), especially concerning relations between Judaizing Christians and Gentile Christians; (2) to obtain the assistance of the Church of Rome in financing a missionary voyage to Spain (see 15:28). Of these two objectives, the first is of course the most important. Paul urgently wishes to present the point of view that he has arrived at as a result of his conflicts with his Corinthian and Galatian adversaries. That is why certain subjects that had been treated only partially or even by an oblique reference in the earlier letters are developed more carefully in this Letter to the Romans.

Indications as to the place of Romans in the chronology of Paul's travels are provided by (1) the passage where he declares that he has wanted for a very long time to pay a visit to the Christians of Rome (see 1:10–15); (2) the one where he states that he has preached the gospel as far as Illyria (i.e., on the east coast of the Adriatic); (3) his intention to travel to Jerusalem bringing the sums offered by the churches of Macedonia and Achaia (see 15:25); (4) the fact that he commends Phoebe, a "deaconess" from Cenchreae, one of the ports of Corinth. These indications suggest that the letter was written from Corinth during the winter 57–58 or from Neapolis, at the moment when Paul was about to set sail for Syria and Palestine, in the spring of 58.

The Letter to the Romans is like the apostle's last will and testament, and it allows us to understand very clearly how Paul himself understood his gospel: the freedom of Christianity as opposed to the particularistic and national religion of the Jews, but also the perfect fulfillment of that religion in the universal religion now liberated from the Law. "The gospel...is the power of God for salvation to every one who has faith" (1:16); this is the apostle's main theme, to which all the other ideas are subordinate.

The letter begins with a proclamation of the universal righteousness of God (see 1:1–17), as contrasted with the universality of sin and guilt (see 1:18; 3:20). God has just demonstrated his righteousness by Christ's sacrifice (see 3:21–31), by the fulfillment of the promise that he made to Abraham (see 4:13–25), for the benefit of sinners, sons of Adam (see 5:12–21), who die at baptism so as to be reborn with Christ (see 6:1–14); the human condition of interior conflict (see 7:13–25) is transformed by God, who gives new life in the Spirit (see 8: 1–17). This chapter ends with the song of triumph about the assurance of salvation (8:35, 38–39).

Who shall separate us from the love of Christ? Shall tribulation, or distress, or persecution, or famine, or nakedness, or peril, or sword?...

> For I am sure that neither death, nor life, nor angels,
> nor principalities, nor things present, nor things to come,
> nor powers, nor height, nor depth, nor anything else in all
> creation, will be able to separate us from the love of God
> in Christ Jesus our Lord.

But does this mean that God is being unjust toward
the Jewish people as a whole? No, because this people has
strayed only for a time; when all the Gentiles are saved,
Israel will be saved in turn (see chapters 9–11).

In the second part of the letter (see 12:1–15 and chap.
13), which is usually called the moral section, Paul speaks
about the life based on love. This charity is, in the first
place, the bond that unites all the members of the Mystical Body of Christ, the Church (see 12:1–8). In Christ we
form one body; hence the need for fraternal charity, which
guarantees good order in society, since the social order
depends on acceptance of the fact that all authority comes
from God and that we owe him obedience.

The Letter to the Romans ends with a longer epi-
logue than usual (see 15:14—16:27), perhaps because of
the importance of the Christian community in the capital
of the empire. Paul explains why he had written this letter and describes his personal plans. His final words are
a splendid hymn of praise to God through Jesus Christ
(16:25–27).

> Now to him who is able to strengthen you according to
> my gospel and the preaching of Jesus Christ, according to
> the revelation of the mystery which was kept secret for
> long ages but is now disclosed and through the prophetic
> writings is made known to all nations, according to the
> command of the eternal God, to bring about the obedience
> of faith—*to the only wise God be glory for evermore through
> Jesus Christ! Amen* [italics added].

While he was waiting for the first boat sailing east that would take him to Jerusalem, Paul learned that the Jews had hatched a plot to get rid of him, once and for all. There is no doubt whatsoever that his enemies would have assassinated him in his sleep and thrown his body overboard. Paul thwarted this attempt by making a detour via Macedonia.

He was accompanied on this voyage to Asia by Sopater, son of Pyrrhus of Beroea; the Thessalonians were represented by Aristarchus and Secundus; then came Gaius of Derbe, Timothy from Lystra, and from the proconsular province of Asia: Tychicus and Trophimus. They had all departed earlier and were waiting for Paul in Troas.

After the days of Unleavened Bread that followed Passover in the year 58, Paul and Luke left Philippi and embarked at Neapolis for Alexandria Troas, where they stayed for a week.

At the end of their stay, the disciples gathered to break bread and to listen to Paul. He gave a long speech that extended well past midnight. Many lamps illuminated the upper room where they had gathered. Now a young man named Eutychus ("lucky" in Greek) was seated on a windowsill; he fell into a deep sleep and fell out into the night. He was found on the ground lifeless; Paul went downstairs and bent over him, embraced him, and said, "Do not be alarmed, for his life is in him" (Acts 20:10). After Paul ascended once more to the meeting room, he spoke again for a long time until dawn and then departed.

And the lucky young man was among them, quite alive, which was a great consolation for the congregation.

From Troas to Miletus

Paul's companions doubled the Cape of Lectum while Paul, on foot, left the city by the southern gate. Skirting the hot springs, he walked through the holm oak forest so as to arrive in Assos by the Sacred Way. This was a long day's walk. The city was perched quite high on its cliff, and the descent to the port was so steep and so dangerous that Stratonicus ironically commented:

> *If you want a premature death,*
> *Make haste and go to Assos.*

The [philosopher-]poet Cleanthes had been born in that city 350 years earlier, and this was the site of the famous sarcophagus that consumed whole bodies, except for the teeth, in less than forty days.

At Assos "we took him [Paul] on board" the boat (Acts 20:14), which that afternoon reached the port of Mytilene, the capital of the island of Lesbos, fatherland of Alcaeus and Sappho, both of them poets. It was also the birthplace of Pittacus, one of the Seven Sages of Greece. The great Aristoteles came to Mytilene to study for two years with the famous learned men of his time.

Paul and his companions set out to sea again the next day and put into port at the isle of Chios, which is renowned for its wine, its marble, and for being one of the many places that claimed the honor and privilege of being the birthplace of Homer.

The following day, the coast of Ionia appeared along with the imposing port of Ephesus. The ship did not stop there but steered for Samos, which also produced a famous wine: "Fill to the brim the cup of wine from Samos."

The tyrant Polycrates, thanks to his magic ring, succeeded at everything that he undertook, until the day when he was taken prisoner and crucified by the satrap of Sardis, who was subject to Persia. Pythagoras was born in Samos; disgusted by Polycrates' tyranny, he decided to immigrate to Croton in Italy and founded there his school, from which came Empedocles and also Philolaus. The latter sold the books of the school to Plato. It was also the place of residence of the lyric poet Simonides, who sang of Marathon, Thermopylae, the Artemisium, and Salamis. He won his fifty-fifth honorary prize at the age of eighty.

The next day, toward noon, they reached Miletus, some thirty-seven miles from Ephesus, where the river Meander "meanders" to the sea. For a brief time it was the capital of Ionia, the mother of eighty colonies, and in the period that we are dealing with it was a city of some importance. It was the fatherland of Thales, another one of the Seven Sages. He was the teacher of Anaximander, who became the teacher of Anaximenes, who had Anaxagoras as a disciple. The last mentioned traveled to Athens, where he had Pericles and Euripides as pupils. The city was famous for its woolen goods and its theater. It was also notorious for its licentious songs and its forthright speech.

Paul seems to have avoided Ephesus, no doubt because of the many enemies who lived there, but above all to hasten his arrival in Jerusalem, which he wanted to reach before Pentecost of the year 58. But he could not ignore Ephesus completely. From Miletus he sent for the elders of the Church, who presented themselves two days later. He gave them a touching farewell speech.

> You yourselves know how I lived among you all the time from the first day that I set foot in Asia, serving the Lord with all humility and with tears and with trials which befell me through the plots of the Jews; how I did not shrink from declaring to you anything that was profitable, and teaching you in public and from house to house, testifying both to Jews and to Greeks of repentance to God and of faith in our Lord Jesus Christ. And now, behold, I am going to Jerusalem, bound in the Spirit, not knowing what shall befall me there; except that the Holy Spirit testifies

to me in every city that imprisonment and afflictions await me. . . . And now, behold, I know that all you among whom I have gone about preaching the kingdom will see my face no more. . . . And now I commend you to God and to the word of his grace, which is able to build you up and to give you the inheritance among all those who are sanctified." (Acts 20:17–23, 25, 32)

After this discourse, Paul knelt down and prayed with them. And they all burst into tears and embraced him, covering him with kisses, lamenting especially the fact that he had said that they would not see his face again. And they accompanied him to the ship.

From Miletus to Jerusalem

Tearing themselves away from their friends, Paul and his companions reached the Island of Cos, a real Garden of Eden, famous for its pottery, wines, silken goods, and ointments. It was a very special place for Luke. Indeed, the island housed the great medical school of Aesculapius and was also the birthplace of Hippocrates, the most famous physician of antiquity. There the mariners lowered the sail for the night.

Opposite Cos, in the bay of Halicarnassus, the fleet of Xanthippus crushed the Persian navy in the month of September of the year 479 B.C.

At daybreak they rounded the cape of Cnidos, famous for its Venus by Praxiteles, and arrived at Rhodes, "the land of roses".

The city had been built by Hippodamus, who had laid out the streets of Piraeus; it was famous especially for its shipyards. Herod the Great had a temple to Apollo built there, the famous Pythium. Among the three thousand statues in the city was the Colossus of Rhodes, a statue of

Helios that was almost one hundred feet high and one of the Seven Wonders of the World. It had been constructed by Chares of Lindum almost three hundred years before. Fifty years later, an earthquake brought down the statue, and Paul could see only the legs that remained intact on the pedestal, while the rest of that enormous body made of bronze lay in the port.

On a sunny morning, the eight peaks of the mountains in the Cragus chain could be seen to the north, and soon the ship skirted the seven capes that jut into the sea from the green slopes of the enormous massif. Shortly afterward they entered the yellowish mouth of the river Xanthus (Xanthos means yellow in Greek), with the city and the port of Patara nestled among the palm trees, in the midst of which a visitor discovered the famous temple of Apollo as well as the theater hewn in the rock. They disembarked and took a boat that was setting sail for Tyre. This was a 340-mile crossing that could be made in four days in good weather and with a favorable wind, leaving Cyprus on the port side without stopping there.

Tyre is mentioned in the Old Testament in connection with Jonah's great adventure. That is where the whale threw him back onto the sand. King Hiram ordered breakwaters built for the port and provided the cedars of Lebanon for the construction of Solomon's Temple (see 1 Kings 5:10). For thirteen long years Nebuchadnezzar besieged the city, which was well protected on its island, and finally was forced to sign a peace treaty with the Tyrians. There Ahab married Jezebel, the daughter of the king of the Sidonians (see 1 Kings 16:29–30). Ezekiel prophesied the ruin of this wealthy, beautiful city (see Ezek 27 and 28). Alexander the Great constructed a pier 875 yards long so as to seize the place; after a siege lasting seven months it became the unfortunate victim of his pent-up rage. Christ visited the nearby coast and mentioned the city in his warning about the Last Judgment (see Mt 11:21; 15:21).

From Tyre the ship scudded along toward Ptolemais, one of the most ancient ports in the world, mentioned in Judges 1:31 by the name of Acco; the Egyptians besieged it before the days of Joseph. Sennacherib and Esarhaddon attacked the city with significant forces without being able to conquer it. Cleopatra was its queen; Vespasian and Titus seized it. The Crusaders, under Baldwin I and Richard the Lionhearted, knew it by the name of Saint John of Acre and carried it by storm. In 1799 Napoleon Bonaparte bombarded it in vain and had to retreat. In this famous port Paul spent one day with the Christians of the city.

The next day they landed at Caesarea Maritima, Caesarea Stratonis, where they were welcomed at the house of Philip, one of the seven first deacons. Philip had four daughters who prophesied (see Acts 6:5; 21:8–9).

While they were staying for a few days in Caesarea, a certain prophet by the name of Agabus arrived from Judea. He made contact with the disciples and, going up to Paul, took his sash and bound his own hands and feet with it saying, "Thus says the Holy Spirit, 'So shall the Jews at Jerusalem bind the man who owns this belt and deliver him into the hands of the Gentiles'" (Acts 21:11).

When the disciples and the men from Galilee heard these words, they begged Paul not to go to Jerusalem. "Then Paul answered, 'What are you doing, weeping and breaking my heart? For I am ready not only to be imprisoned but even to die at Jerusalem for the name of the Lord Jesus.' And when he would not be persuaded, we ceased and said, 'The will of the Lord be done'" (21:13–14).

Several days later the travelers packed their bags and set out in caravan on the road to Jerusalem, which was around sixty miles distant. They were accompanied by several believers from Caesarea, who entrusted them to Mnason of Cyprus, a disciple from the earliest days (see Acts 21:16), with whom they found lodgings. The next day Paul arrived in the holy city of the Jews, just in time for the celebration of Pentecost.

10

Arrest and Imprisonment in Caesarea

When Paul arrived in Jerusalem for Pentecost in the month of May, A.D. 58, the brethren were very glad to welcome him. The following day he had an interview with James, the apostle who was revered by all. All the elders were present. Paul greeted them and explained to them in detail everything that the Lord had accomplished through his labors among the Gentiles. As fruits of his efforts he could point to his traveling companions, all of them now disciples of Christ, although they originally came from many cities.

It was a beautiful moment for Paul and his companions to be able, as a group, to present the offerings collected among the converts from paganism for benefit of the Christian community in Jerusalem, from which the gospel of salvation came to them.

In response, James and the elders effusively expressed their gratitude and offered prayers of thanksgiving. But James, speaking to Paul, hastened to add, "You see, brother, how many thousands there are among the Jews of those who have believed; they are all zealous for the law, and they have been told about you that you teach all the Jews who are among the Gentiles to forsake Moses, telling them not to circumcise their children or observe the customs. What then is to be done? They will certainly hear that you have come" (Acts 21:20–22). It could lead to an accusation, violence, or perhaps even death. What did Paul think of that?!

James had a solution all ready: "We have four men who are under a vow; take these men and purify yourself along with them and pay their expenses, so that they may shave their heads. Thus all will know that there is nothing in what they have been told about you but that you yourself live in observance of the law" (21:23–24).

Paying the expenses of poor "Nazirites" was, among the Jews of that era, an act of charity. But James' proposal went against everything that Paul had accomplished thus far. It was not a question of principle but rather of prudence, a matter of patience with the needs of the Jewish Christians, and therefore Paul followed the advice of James. He agreed so as not to poison a situation that was already so strained. Paul went therefore to the court of the Temple, after purifying himself, to announce when the days of the Nazirite vow would be completed, and he remained there until the sacrifice had been offered for each one of them.

When the seven days were drawing to a close, the Jews of the province of Asia, having seen Paul in the Temple, stirred up the people, "crying out, 'Men of Israel, help! This is the man who is teaching men everywhere against the people and the law and this place; moreover he also brought Greeks into the temple, and he has defiled this holy place.' For they had previously seen Trophimus the Ephesian with him in the city, and they supposed that Paul had brought him into the temple" (Acts 21:28–29).

In collaboration with the *"Société d'Exploration de la Palestine"*, the Frenchman Clément Ganneau discovered along the Via Dolorosa the inscription quoted in chapter 3 (p. 36 above). It was a formal prohibition forbidding any pagan under pain of death to enter the inner precincts of the Temple.

Paul certainly never had intended to bring a Gentile into the forbidden part of the Temple. But the accusation was crafty. It provided a good excuse to get rid of Paul according to the Jewish law, without the intervention of the Roman authorities. According to Flavius Josephus, this right of theirs was still honored by the emperor Titus several years later. The crowd was swelling visibly; the people might have stoned Paul on the spot, but they were standing within the precincts of the holy place, and they would have to take him outside the Temple first and close the doors before proceeding to an execution.

From the top of the Tower of Antony at the northwest corner of the Temple, the sentinel on guard saw the menacing throng and sounded the alarm. The tribune Claudius Lysias, together with a powerful escort, immediately confronted the populace. At the sight of the centurions and soldiers, they stopped beating Paul. The tribune approached and put his hand on Paul, signaling that no one else could touch him; he had him bound with two chains to two soldiers who were ordered to let themselves be killed rather than allow him to escape or anyone else to make an attempt on his life. For he was now a prisoner of Rome.

Turning to the multitude, Lysias asked who this man was whom they wanted to lynch, and what crime he had committed. But in the crowd some shouted this, and others that. Unable to get to the bottom of it in the confusion, he ordered them to take the arrested man away to the fortress. The crowd, shouting for his death, was so violent that Paul had to be carried by the soldiers. As it had crucified Christ less than thirty years earlier, now it wanted to stone the apostle of Christ.

Paul's Defense

As they entered the fortress, Paul turned to the tribune and said to him, "May I say something to you?" "Do you know Greek?" the tribune replied in astonishment. "Are you not the Egyptian, then, who recently stirred up a revolt and led the four thousand men of the Assassins out into the wilderness?" (Acts 21:37–38). These were sicarii, "men armed with a dagger".

"I am a Jew, from Tarsus in Cilicia, a citizen of no mean city; I beg you, let me speak to the people" (21:39). When the tribune gave him permission, Paul stood on the steps and stretched out his hand, a sign that he wanted to speak. A profound silence ensued. Then, using the Hebrew (or Aramaic) language, he spoke to them as follows: "Brethren and fathers, hear the defense which I now make before you." (22:1). In this connection Saint John Chrysostom wrote, "What nobler spectacle than that of Paul at that moment. There he stood, bound by two chains, ready to defend himself before the people. The Roman commander seated beside him guaranteed security by his presence. An enraged crowd looked at him from below. And yet, in the midst of these dangers, what assurance, what calm!"

Paul spoke about his birth and training as a Pharisee, remarking that he was "zealous for God as you all are this day" (22:3). He mentions that he once persecuted to the death the "Way" (22:4), the Christians, a fact to which the high priest and all the elders could testify. He recounted also his conversion and the instruction that was given him by the Lord: "Depart; for I will send you far away to the Gentiles" (22:21).

The Jews had listened to him until then in silence, but at these words they made their voices heard: "Away with such a fellow from the earth! For he ought not to live!" And they cried out, waving their mantles in the air and throwing dust, acting like madmen. To avoid the worst, the tribune ordered that Paul be brought inside the fortress to be scourged and questioned so as to know why they were shouting against him like that. And as they were tying him to the pillar, Paul said to the centurion, "Is it lawful for you to scourge a man who is a Roman citizen, and uncondemned?" When these words were repeated to the tribune, he hurried over to Paul and said to him, "Are you a Roman citizen?" "Yes", he answered. And the tribune continued, "I bought this citizenship for a large sum" (22:22, 25, 27, 28).

Judging by his name, the tribune had purchased his citizenship through an intermediary, the wife of the emperor Claudius, who had profited greatly by this scheme, as Dio Cassius relates. Paul replied with some pride in his voice, "But I was born a citizen" (22:28). A great silence ensued while the tribune, astounded, stared at the apostle. One can imagine Luke's smile as he wrote this dialogue down in Acts.

Cicero, in his *Contra Verrem*, tells us that "it is a great injustice to bind a Roman citizen; it is an atrocity to scourge him; it is a crime approaching parricide to deprive him of life and, I might add, to crucify him."

Immediately the executioners withdrew and the tribune wondered how he could get out of this thorny predicament. Indeed, he had had Paul bound and ordered him tortured contrary to the formal prohibition of Roman law. And Cicero reminds us, "How many times the exclamation, 'I am a Roman citizen,' has brought help and safety, even among the barbarians, to the remotest places on earth."

Paul Brought before the Sanhedrin

The next day, wishing to know exactly what charges the Jews were leveling against Paul, the tribune had his bonds removed, ordered the entire Sanhedrin to assemble, and had Paul brought down into their midst. The emperor Caligula, indeed, had granted to the Sanhedrin the right to judge all strictly religious cases throughout his territory.

Paul had his eyes fixed on the Sanhedrin. The apostles Peter and John had preceded him there on the occasion when Gamaliel had recommended setting them free, and in that same place Stephen had been condemned to death. Paul in turn found himself accused at the tribunal of the Sanhedrin; perhaps he saw there Simon and Joshua, the sons of his teacher Gamaliel.

Paul began, "Brethren, I have lived before God in all good conscience up to this day." At these words the high priest Ananias ordered one of the attendants to strike him on the mouth. Paul, highly offended by this treatment, did not mince words: "God shall strike you, you white-washed wall! Are you sitting to judge me according to the law, and yet contrary to the law you order me to be struck?" The attendants replied, "Would you revile God's High Priest?" Paul, somewhat disconcerted, answered, "I did not know, brethren, that he was the High Priest; for it is written, 'You shall not speak evil of a ruler of your people'" (Acts 23:1, 3–5).

Ananias had been appointed by Herod ten years earlier. In 52 he was accused of fraud by the Samaritans and brought to Rome to be judged. He was acquitted and resumed his duties, holding office for more than eleven years in all—a long time for that era. Since the assembly had been convened in a semiofficial manner, he was not wearing the white robe of the high priest and Paul could not recognize him as such.

Flavius Josephus notes the avarice and cruelty of Ananias. Later on his house was set on fire by a mob organized by his own son. He fled to the countryside but was discovered there and slain by the sicarii.

The Sanhedrin was deeply divided between Sadducees and Pharisees. Paul knew this and took advantage of it. He exclaimed, "Brethren, I am a Pharisee, a son of Pharisees; with respect to the hope and the resurrection of the dead I am on trial" (Acts 23:6). A discussion then arose and the assembly was divided. For the Sadducees believed neither in the resurrection nor in angels, nor in spirits. But the Pharisees considered them to be real.

There was a great commotion, and several scribes of the Pharisee party argued vehemently, saying, "We find nothing wrong in this man. What if a spirit or an angel spoke to him?" (23:9). As the clamor grew louder, the tribune, fearing that Paul might be torn to pieces, and perhaps recalling the Latin proverb "truth is lost in the midst of disputes", ordered the soldiers to go down and take him away and bring him back into the fortress.

That night the Lord appeared to Paul and said to him, "Take courage, for as you have testified about me at Jerusalem, so you must bear witness also at Rome" (23:11).

At daybreak a group of Jews devised a plot and swore not to eat or drink as long as Paul remained alive. More than forty men were involved in the conspiracy. They went to the chief priests and the elders, saying, "We have strictly bound ourselves by an oath to taste no food till we have killed Paul. You therefore, along with the council, give notice now to the tribune to bring him down to you, as though you were going to determine his case more exactly. And we are ready to kill him before he comes near" (23:14–15).

We can only be astonished by their attitude, but that way of doing things was perfectly acceptable in those days. It was legal, among the Jews, for a private person to liquidate someone who had abandoned the Law of Moses, and this was the accusation being leveled at Paul. Flavius Josephus relates that some Jews had sworn to assassinate Herod as an apostate from the Jewish law. Philo of Alexandria, the great Jewish philosopher, wrote, "It is quite fitting that all who are zealous for virtue should have the right to punish, with their own hands and without delay, those who are guilty of that crime", namely, apostasy from Judaism.

Paul's nephew caught wind of the plot and ran to the fortress to tell Paul, who, through the agency of a centurion, sent the boy to the tribune to inform him of the conspiracy. The latter sent the young man back after advising him to tell no one about what he had communicated to him.

Lysias called two centurions: "At the third hour of the night [9:00 p.m.] get ready two hundred soldiers with seventy horsemen and two hundred spearmen to go as far as Caesarea. Also provide mounts for Paul to ride, and bring him safely to Felix the governor" (Acts 23:23–24).

Then he wrote his elogium, or judiciary report, as follows:

> Claudius Lysias to his Excellency the governor Felix, greeting. This man was seized by the Jews, and was about to be killed by them, when I came upon them with the soldiers and rescued him, having learned that he was a Roman citizen. And desiring to know the charge on which they accused him, I brought him down to their council. I found that he was accused about questions of their law, but charged with nothing deserving death or imprisonment. And when it was disclosed to me that there would be a plot against the man, I sent him to you at once, ordering his accusers also to state before you what they have against him. [Farewell.] (23:26–30)

The tribune Claudius was without a doubt an excellent high-ranking Roman official; he was also a very diplomatic letter writer. He very conveniently "forgot" to mention that he had arrested Paul, mistaking him for a notorious rebel. He passed over in silence the order that he had given to have Paul—a Roman citizen—beaten with rods; he tries to make it appear that he came to the aid of Paul in the latter's capacity as a Roman citizen, although he learned about it only later. Despite all that, Claudius showed some sympathy for Paul and assuredly saved his life by a swift and decisive intervention.

The soldiers set out at night and led Paul as far as Antipatris, a real paradise. At the *gallicinium*, the cockcrow, the foot soldiers returned to Jerusalem, while the horsemen continued down the road with the prisoner. At Caesarea the governor Felix read the letter and, learning from Paul that he was from Cilicia, said, "I will hear you when your accusers arrive." And he ordered him to be guarded in Herod's praetorium. It was June of A.D. 58.

Herod had transformed the little fishing port known as "Strato's Tower" into a beautiful city named Caesarea in honor of Augustus. He had the plan drawn up for it, and the city was built in less than twelve years. The buildings were made of marble, the private houses as well as the palaces. But the real masterpiece was the spacious port, larger than the Piraeus of Athens, a harbor shielded from the winds and the storms.

Famous for its port, Caesarea Stratonis became the port of Jerusalem. The new road, about sixty-two miles long, was paved in the Roman manner. Aqueducts brought water from Mount Carmel, twenty-five miles away, and from the nearby river.

Herod did not fail to dedicate a temple to Augustus, remarkable for its splendor and its dimensions, which was topped by a colossal statue of the emperor, in imitation of and no less imposing than the one of Jupiter Olympus, and by another statue of the goddess Roma. Herod also built a forum, a stadium, and an amphitheater, not to mention a sumptuous palace. The city was dedicated in the year 10 B.C.

Herod Agrippa I left Jerusalem and went to Caesarea for a series of games to celebrate the triumphant return of the emperor Claudius after his glorious victories in Britannia, modern-day England. Here he received the envoys from Sidon and Tyre who were suing for peace. On the appointed day Herod, dressed in sumptuous royal vesture and seated on a throne, harangued them while the people proclaimed, "[It is] the voice of a god, and not of [a] man!" (Acts 12:22). At that very moment an angel of the Lord struck him because he had not given glory to God. And he died consumed by worms.

Within the city there were several important synagogues, and the Jews were so numerous that twenty thousand of them were massacred by Titus after the destruction of Jerusalem.

Herod's palace was also the residence and the praetorium of the Roman government of Judea. Within the palace there was a prison, where Paul stayed during his incarceration at Caesarea.

Paul Brought before Felix

Claudius had become emperor, thanks to the efforts of King Agrippa II; he was therefore well disposed toward the Jews and ordered the Roman magistrates to respect their worship. When the chief priest Jonathan and Agrippina lent their support to Antonius Felix as governor of Judea, Claudius expedited the appointment and made it for a period of seven years, from 52 to 59, instead of the usual two or three years.

Unfortunately, Felix proved to be a tyrant. He put down a rebellion with extreme cruelty. And when the chief priest Jonathan protested against that outrage, Felix had him assassinated in the Temple precincts.

His private life was equally lamentable. That unscrupulous freedman, Suetonius tells us, had been the husband of three queens. We know nothing about the first one; the second was Drusilla, the daughter of the king of Mauritania and the granddaughter of Antony and Cleopatra; the third, another Drusilla, sister of King Agrippa II, was the wife of the king of Emesa, Syria. The charms of this beautiful Jewess attracted the attention of Felix, who used the magician Simon of Cyprus to convince her to forsake her husband and marry Felix. Felix and Drusilla lived at that time in Caesarea Philippi.

Tacitus writes, "Antonius Felix, indulging in every kind of barbarity and lust, exercised the power of a king in the spirit of a slave" (*Annals* 12, 54; *Histories* 5, 9). He did not think it necessary to curb his passions but considered that his tie with his brother Pallas, the emperor's favorite, gave him license to commit the worst crimes. That was the judge before whom Paul was going to appear.

The Roman tribunals administered justice promptly. And so five days after Paul's arrival in Caesarea, the high priest Ananias and his assistants, accompanied by an advocate named Tertullus, who was probably from Italy originally, presented themselves to lodge a complaint against Paul.

Tertullus presented the plaintiff's arguments. He did so very cleverly. If he omitted the usual compliments, he would offend the judge; if he praised the judge excessively, he would displease his clients, who hated Felix. He prudently contented himself with praising the governor for the order prevailing in his province. "Since through you we enjoy much peace, and since by your provision, most excellent Felix, reforms are introduced on behalf of this nation, in every way and everywhere we accept this with all gratitude. But, to detain you no further, I beg you in your kindness to hear us briefly" (Acts 24:2–4).

1. "We have found this man a pestilent fellow, an agitator among all the Jews throughout the world" (24:5). He was

charged first with having made a serious attack on Roman authority; it was tantamount to a crime of high treason and put Paul in a perilous situation.

2. "A ringleader of the sect of the Nazarenes" (24:5). And therefore a sectarian.

3. " 'He even tried to profane the temple, but we seized him, and we would have judged him according to our law. But the chief captain Lysias came and with great violence took him out of our hands, commanding his accusers to come before you. By examining him yourself you will be able to learn from him about everything of which we accuse him.' The Jews also joined in the charge, affirming that all this was so" (24:6–9).

At a sign from the governor, Paul stood up to present his defense (see 24:10–21).

"Realizing that for many years you have been judge over this nation, I cheerfully make my defense" (24:10).

After this tactful, truthful introduction, Paul responded to the charges brought against him, one by one.

1. *Sedition.* "It is not more than twelve days since I went up to worship at Jerusalem; and they did not find me disputing with any one or stirring up a crowd, either in the Temple or in the synagogues, or in the city. Neither can they prove to you what they now bring up against me" (24:11–13).

Only twelve days, and five of them under arrest! That is hardly time enough to organize an insurrection. Absurd! A simple exposition of the facts refutes the accusation.

2. *Sectarianism.* "But this I admit to you, that according to the Way, which they call a sect, I worship the God of our fathers, believing everything laid down by the law or written in the prophets, having a hope in God which these themselves accept, that there will be a resurrection of both the just and the unjust. So I always take pains to have a clear conscience toward God and toward men" (24:14–16).

3. *Sacrilege.* "Now after some years I came to bring to my nation alms and offerings. As I was doing this, they found me purified in the temple, without any crowd or tumult. But some Jews from Asia—they ought to be here before you and to make an accusation, if they have anything against me. Or else let these men themselves say what wrongdoing they found when I stood before the council [i.e., the Sanhedrin]" (24:19–20).

Felix knew that the accusation was false; Paul was innocent and his verdict ought to have been: "I declare the accused innocent; set him free!"

But no! In order to please the Jews, Felix adjourned the case, alleging that "when Lysias the tribune comes down, I will decide your case" (24:22). Then he ordered the centurion to guard Paul while allowing him some freedom and authorizing him to see his friends. Philip the deacon and many others visited him.

Paul's attitude and speech made a great impression on Felix. And so, several days later, accompanied by Drusilla, he summoned him to hear him speak about faith in Jesus the Christ. Paul eventually spoke about justice, temperance, and the future judgment. Felix, alarmed, interrupted him: "Go away for the present; when I have an opportunity I will summon you" (24:25). At the same time he hoped that Paul would offer him some money; and so he sent for him frequently, to converse with him. This was quite contrary to the *Lex Julia*, which forbade all judges from receiving payment for the imprisonment or liberation of any person whatsoever.

Claudius died in 54, poisoned by the mushrooms served to him by Agrippina, his charming wife. Nero succeeded him. His mistress was Poppaea, a Jewish proselyte, who managed to have Felix called back to Rome. Before leaving Palestine, he kept Paul in prison to please the Jews for the purpose of having the counts of his own indictment reduced. Pallas, his brother, had been banished in 56, and the new treasurer, Claudius Etruscus, hated corrupt officials. Felix escaped capital punishment but found himself compelled to make restitution for his ill-gotten gains. He died as he had begun: without any family, poor, and despised.

Paul Brought before Festus

Porcius Festus, the new governor, arrived in Caesarea during the year 59 and less than three days later went up to Jerusalem to make contact with the people he was getting ready to govern.

The new high priest Ismael and a delegation of Jews lodged a complaint against Paul, asking Festus to send him back to Jerusalem because they wanted to avenge themselves. Festus replied that Paul was being kept in Caesarea and that he himself would return there shortly. "So...let the men of authority among you go down with me, and if there is anything wrong about the man, let them accuse him" (Acts 25:5).

Ten days later Festus returned to Caesarea, and the day after his arrival, having taken his seat, he ordered Paul to be brought before the tribunal. The Jews who had come from Jerusalem made many serious accusations against him, which they were unable to prove. Paul said in his defense: "Neither against the law of the Jews, nor against the temple, nor against Caesar have I offended at all." Festus, who wished to please the Jews, said to Paul, "Do you wish to go up to Jerusalem, and there be tried on these charges before me?" Paul answered him, "I am standing before Caesar's tribunal....If then I am a wrongdoer, and have committed anything for which I deserve to die, I do not seek to escape death; but if there is nothing in their charges against me, no one can give me up to them. [*Kaísara epikaloûmai:*] I appeal to Caesar." Then Festus, after having conferred with his council, answered, "You have appealed to Caesar; to Caesar you shall go" (25:8–12).

Every Roman citizen had the right to appeal to Caesar against the tyranny of provincial magistrates, and the *Lex Julia* forbade any groundless delay in transferring the case to Rome.

Upon the death of Agrippa I, the emperor Claudius had appointed Cuspius Fadus as procurator of Judea, which from that moment on became a Roman province, in A.D. 44. The son of Agrippa I, who was still a minor, had to be content with the little province of Chalcis, along with the right to supervise the Temple and the privilege of appointing the high priest.

The older daughter of Agrippa I, Bernice, was famous for her beauty and notorious for her immorality. She was a widow at the age of twenty-one and lived in an incestuous union with her brother, Agrippa II.

The couple made the journey from Caesarea Philippi to Caesarea Stratonis to pay a visit to the new governor and to congratulate him on his promotion. Several days after their arrival Festus explained Paul's case to the king, saying, "There is a man left prisoner by Felix.... When the accusers stood up, they brought no charge in his case of such evils as I supposed; but they had certain points of dispute with him about their own superstition and about one Jesus, who was dead, but whom Paul asserted to be alive." Agrippa then said to Festus, "I should like to hear the man myself." "Tomorrow," Festus replied, "you shall hear him" (Acts 25:14, 18–19, 22).

The next day Agrippa and Bernice made their entrance into the audience hall with the tribunes and the prominent men of the city. Then Festus said,

> King Agrippa and all who are present with us, you see this
> man about whom the whole Jewish people petitioned me,
> both at Jerusalem and here, shouting that he ought not
> to live any longer. But I found that he had done nothing
> deserving death; and as he himself appealed to the emperor,
> I decided to send him. But I have nothing definite to write
> to my lord about him. Therefore I have brought him before
> you, and, especially before you, King Agrippa, that, after
> we have examined him, I may have something to write.
> (25:24–26)

Paul before Agrippa

Agrippa said to Paul, "You have permission to speak for
yourself." Then Paul, stretching out his hand, justified himself in these terms: "I think myself fortunate that it is before
you, King Agrippa, I am to make my defense today against
all the accusations of the Jews, because you are especially
familiar with all customs and controversies of the Jews;
therefore I beg you to listen to me patiently" (Acts 26:1–3).

These words were not mere flattery on Paul's part or a
simple *captatio benevolentiae* [plea for the listeners' good will].
In rabbinical circles at that time Agrippa II was renowned
for his knowledge of Jewish law.

Paul repeated the story of his youth, his conversion, and
his apostolate among the Gentiles. He added: "To this day
I have had the help that comes from God, and so I stand
here testifying both to small and great, saying nothing but
what the prophets and Moses said would come to pass: that
the Christ must suffer, and that, by being the first to rise
from the dead, he would proclaim light both to the people
and to the Gentiles" (26:22–23).

At these words Festus exclaimed, "Paul, you are mad;
your great learning is turning you mad." But Paul said, "I
am not mad, most excellent Festus, but I am speaking the

sober truth. For the king knows about these things, and to him I speak freely; for I am persuaded that none of these things has escaped his notice, for this was not done in a corner. King Agrippa, do you believe in the prophets? I know that you believe" (26:24–27).

Agrippa replied that in a little more time Paul would make a Christian of him!

"Whether short or long," Paul said, "I would to God that not only you but also all who hear me this day might become such as I am—except for these chains" (26:28–29).

Then the king stood up, and with him the governor, Bernice, and all their attendants. After they had withdrawn, they said to one another, "This man is doing nothing to deserve death or imprisonment." And Agrippa said to Festus, "This man could have been set free if he had not appealed to Caesar" (26:31–32).

Later, at the beginning of the Jewish War, Agrippa welcomed the Christians in his territory and treated them considerately. Had Paul's speech at Caesarea had some effect on him? He belonged to the Roman party, and after the destruction of the Temple of Jerusalem he lived in Rome until his death at the end of the century.

Origen of Alexandria, the great Christian thinker, lived in Caesarea; Eusebius of Caesaria, the Father of Church history, was the local bishop at the beginning of the fourth century. During the first crusade, Baldwin I discovered there the vase of amethyst crystal, which gave rise to the legend about the Holy Grail, the cup which Christ is said to have used at the Last Supper.

11

Voyage to Rome
Crossing and Shipwreck

Toward the end of the year 61, Flavius Josephus took a merchant vessel, *navis oneraria*, that was sailing for Rome with six hundred passengers on board. The ship sank and there were only eighty survivors. At the end of the Jewish War, Titus, the victor, took a merchant vessel also to arrive safe and sound in Puteoli, the large grain shipping center south of Rome.

All these boats departed from Alexandria, Egypt, Caesarea, Sidon, or other ports of Asia Minor, making the great detour via Myra and Rhodes, so as to sail due west toward Sicily and Rome. Why?

The reason was that the prevailing westerly winds made passage in a direct line very difficult and very dangerous. It was much safer to go in a roundabout way via the coasts of Anatolia and then to hug the Greek islands when heading toward Italy.

It was by that circuitous route that Paul, a prisoner of the state, was brought to Rome in the custody of the centurion Julius of the Augustan Cohort, which was part of the Imperial Guard. This was a unit, attached to each legion, that ensured communications between the emperor and his armed forces in the provinces, and that served especially to expedite letters and parcels and to escort high-ranking officials and also prisoners. Its members were known by the name *peregrini*, "foreign legionnaires", and when they arrived in Rome they were quartered in the Castra Peregrinorum on the Caelian Hill, right next to the imperial palace. Aristarchus of Thessalonica and Luke obtained permission to accompany Paul, perhaps thanks to Governor Festus.

In August of 60 they set sail from Caesarea on a ship destined for Adramyttium, a port situated on the Ionian coast, not far from Troas. The following day they put into port at Sidon. Julius proved to be very courteous toward Paul, allowing him to visit his friends in that city and to be cared for. They set sail again and skirted the island of Cyprus because of the contrary winds, and after crossing the sea of Cilicia and Pamphylia, they arrived at Myra, in Lycia, in less than two weeks. Myra was a hub for the grain trade between Egypt and Italy. The city housed the shrine of the god of sailors, to whom they prayed before setting out and made votive offerings after a safe crossing.

There Julius had the good fortune of finding a merchant ship from Alexandria that was departing for Italy; he found room on it for his entire group.

This *navis oneraria* no doubt had a smaller carrying capacity (between four hundred and five hundred tons) than the ship *Goddess Isis*, which, loaded with grain, had been driven back by bad weather toward the port of Piraeus. The Athenians were enraptured by the enormous dimensions of the latter ship.

The Greek historian Lucius (second century after Christ) describes it in *The Ship*.

> What a ship it was! The carpenter tells us that it measured 60 yards in length, 15 yards in width and 14 yards in depth. As for the rest: what a mast! What a sail! What rigging! How graceful its stern, surmounted with a golden goose, the sign that it belonged to the fleet of ships transporting

grain. Each side bears the name of the goddess that is the ship's ensign. And all the rest: the ornamentation, the painting, the banners, especially the anchors, the capstans, the windlasses, and the cabin near the stern; it all seems perfectly marvelous to me. And the multitude of sailors, who could be compared to a small army. They say that the vessel can transport grain in sufficient quantity to feed all Attica for a year. Although this monster is not very tractable, it is commanded by a shriveled old man with a receding hairline who, sitting at the helm, maneuvers with a sort of handle the two heavy oars that serve as a rudder.

For several days the ship transporting Paul made slow progress against a head wind but finally reached Cnidos. At the moment when it was rounding the cape, a wind from the northwest struck and lashed at the boat, forcing the pilot to steer south, under the lee of Crete so as to get past the cape of Salmonetta with difficulty. Laboriously hugging the coast, the ship put into port at a place called Fair Havens, Kaloi Limenes, near the city of Lasaea. There they waited for a favorable wind. But it was late September and the autumn storms were already beginning to make navigation very dangerous.

A council was held. Julius presided, no doubt because of his duties, which connected him with the household of the emperor. Paul, who had traveled much by sea and had been shipwrecked three times, warned the crew, "Sirs, I perceive that the voyage will be with injury and much loss, not only of the cargo and the ship, but also of our lives" (Acts 27:10) But the centurion heeded the opinion of the ship's captain and owner. Moreover the harbor was not a suitable place to winter in. Most of them agreed to put out to sea again and to try to reach the port of Phoenix in order to spend the winter there. It would take only a few hours to sail to that place, beyond Cape Matala.

Storm and Shipwreck

The wind blew from the south and all conditions seemed favorable for a short crossing. The ship left "Fair Havens" and scudded quite close to the shore. But when the pilot was about to pass beyond the cape, a violent northeast wind called Euroclydon, or Euraquilon in Latin, descended from Mount Ida (8,058 feet) and was unleashed on the boat. Unable to fight against the storm, the boat was driven on by the wind. It swiftly passed under the lee of the small island called Cauda. In order to save the vessel and its passengers, the sailors did all they could to secure the boat: they undergirded it to prevent it from breaking up and then, fearing that they would run on the Syrtis, far away in Tripolitania, they lowered the sails and let the boat drift. The next day the situation only got worse; they threw the cargo overboard, then the rigging. There was nothing left to do but to face the exhausting days, the endless nights, gloomy despair and inevitable death. All was lost!

For a long time no one had eaten. Then Paul, emaciated, weakened and bruised like all the others yet full of assurance, stood up and said

> Men, you should have listened to me, and should not have set sail from Crete and incurred this injury and loss. I now bid you take heart; for there will be no loss of life among you, but only of the ship. For this very night there stood by me an angel of the God to whom I belong and whom I worship, and he said, "Do not be afraid, Paul; you must stand before Caesar; and behold, God has granted you all those who sail with you." So take heart, men, for I have faith in God that it will be exactly as I have been told. (Acts 27:21–25)

At that moment, perhaps, Paul remembered Psalm 46(45) and recited it fervently with his two companions:

God is our refuge and strength,
  a very present help in trouble.
Therefore we will not fear though the earth should
    change, though the mountains shake in the heart
    of the sea;
though its waters roar and foam,
  though the mountains tremble with its tumult.

(Ps 46:1–3)

On the fourteenth night, while they continued to be
tossed about on the Adriatic, the sailors suspected that they
were nearing land. So they sounded and found twenty fathoms (120 feet). A little farther they sounded again and found
fifteen fathoms. Afraid that they might be dashed on the
rocks, they let out four anchors from the stern and waited
for daylight. How impatiently! However, as the sailors were
trying to desert the ship and had lowered the ship's boat
into the sea, under pretense of laying out anchors from
the bow, Paul, always on the alert, told the centurion and
the soldiers, "Unless these men stay in the ship, you cannot
be saved" (Acts 27:31). Immediately, unsheathing their short
swords, they cut the ropes of the boat and let it go.

While waiting for daybreak, Paul exhorted everyone to
eat something.

> "Today is the fourteenth day that you have continued
> in suspense and without food, having taken nothing.
> Therefore I urge you to take some food; it will give you
> strength, since not a hair is to perish from the head of any
> of you." And when he had said this, he took bread, and
> giving thanks to God in the presence of all, he broke it
> and began to eat. Then they all were encouraged and ate
> some food themselves. (27:33–36)

When the sullen dawn finally appeared, they all spied a
bay with a sandy beach, and they decided to run the ship

aground. They cut the cables of the anchors and at the same time loosened the ropes that tied the rudders; hoisting the foresail to the wind, they made for the beach. When they struck a shoal between two currents separating the island of Salmonetta from the northeast shore of the island, the ship ran aground. The bow stuck and remained immovable, and the stern was broken up by the violent waves.

The soldiers intended to kill the prisoners, for fear that one of them might swim away and escape. But the centurion, wishing to save Paul, was opposed to their plan. He ordered those who knew how to swim to make for land first, and the rest to cling to planks or debris from the ship. And in that way they all got to shore safe and sound, soldiers and sailors, passengers and prisoners, sinners and saints: 266 persons in all.

They very quickly discovered that the island was called Melita (Malta), and they were welcomed kindly by the inhabitants, around a great fire that they had lit because of the rain and the cold.

Paul, indefatigable, had gathered some sticks, and when he threw them on the fire a viper came out because of the heat and fastened on his hand. Seeing the reptile hanging from his hand, the inhabitants said to one another, "No doubt this man is a murderer. Though he has escaped from the sea, justice has not allowed him to live." They expected to see him swell up and fall down dead. But after a long wait, seeing that no harm had come to him, "they changed their minds and said that he was a god" (Acts 28:4, 6).

Publius, the *protos*, or "chief", of the island, no doubt a delegate of the governor of Sicily, welcomed and lodged the shipwrecked party for three days. Publius' father was in bed, sick with fever and dysentery. Paul visited him and, after praying, imposed hands on him and healed him.

Healing Prayer

Thereupon all the other sick people of the locality came to see him and were healed.

After staying for three months, from mid-November to mid-February of A.D. 61, the shipwrecked party boarded a ship that had spent the winter on the island. It was the Dioscuri, named after Castor and Pollux, the twin sons of Jupiter and Leda, who were transported into the heavens to form the constellation Gemini. They were reputed to have a beneficent influence on the sea, and that is why they were the tutelary gods of mariners.

At the first favorable wind they went to sea again. After making an eighty-seven mile crossing without incident, the vessel put into port for three days at Syracuse, the city of the five towns, which rivaled Carthage in wealth, according to Strabo. Cicero calls it "glorious Syracuse, the largest and most beautiful of Greek cities". It was a colony of Corinth and for many years "almost" the mistress of the world.

An old tradition tells us that Christianity was introduced to Syracuse in 44 by a man named Marcian and that Paul preached in the temple of Dionysius, which became the Church of St. John. The temple of Minerva, praised by Cicero for its beauty, is presently the cathedral. Beyond Syracuse, Paul did not fail to notice a strange, active volcano, an immense, near-perfect cone, Mount Etna, with its snow-covered summit crowned with sulfuric vapors.

The ship stopped over for a day at Rhegium (Reggio di Calabria). Within the city there is an impressive cathedral bearing the inscription *Katèntèsamen eis Règôn*, "We arrived at Rhegium" (see Acts 28:13). Fifteen miles from the city, aided by a strong southerly wind, the boat cleared the Fretum Siculum, the famous Strait of Sicily, with Charybdis on the Sicilian coast and Scylla—a girl whom Circe jealously turned into a rock that imperiled navigation—on the Italian coast of Bruttium [Calabria]. A little farther on, Paul

could see Stromboli with its active volcano in the midst
of the Lipari Islands. Several hours later, and there was
the island of Capreae or Capri, famous for its blue grotto,
the dwelling place of the Sirens and the residence of the
Caesars. There Augustus constructed palaces and baths, had
aqueducts built, and spent the final years of his life. His
successor, Tiberius, settled there as of the year A.D. 27 and
left behind a sinister reputation.

The ship rounded the promontory of Sorrentum, which
was topped by the temple of Minerva, and there, before the
eyes of the astonished passengers, was revealed the Bay of
Naples, one of the most beautiful in the world. The ancients
called it *Parthénope* after a siren that had emerged from the
waves. To the left they could discern the cape of Misenum,
where Lucullus had his famous villa and where Tiberius
gave up the ghost, suffocated under blankets at the order
of the prefect Naevius Sertorius Macro, who thought that
he was agonizing too slowly. It was also the home port of
the Roman fleet. Dominating the bay, at the center, rose
majestic Vesuvius, dormant at that time and covered with
vineyards as far as the summit. It was here that Pliny the
Younger, on August 24, A.D. 79, observed the sudden erup-
tion of the volcano and the destruction of Pompeii on the
right and of Herculaneum to the left.

At the back of the bay the Greeks had founded Neapolis,
the "New City", with its famous green hill of Posillipo,
where Cicero had his villa; so did Virgil, who composed
his *Georgics* and *Aeneid* there.

The bay and the port of Puteoli, in Italian Pozzuoli, or
in Greek Dicaearchia, situated 9 miles to the northwest of
Naples, was the most important port in Italy, especially for
supplying grain to Rome, which was 140 miles away. There
they had built a pier consisting of twenty-five arches, fifteen
of which are still visible today, where the ships unloaded

their cargo. At the arrival of a huge Egyptian grain boat, which could carry up to twelve hundred tons, a curious crowd came to admire the spectacle. Seneca, in one of his letters, describes the scene for us:

> Quite unexpectedly today, swift Alexandrian boats appeared to announce the arrival of the fleet. They are called "packet boats", because they carry letters and packages; their arrival is welcomed in all Campania. The crowd presses on the pier of Puteoli and identifies the Alexandrian grain ships, amid all the others, by their sails, for they alone have permission to enter the port with the "topgallant sail", the topsail unfurled.... At that moment the whole city comes to the port to see the sailors dancing for joy on the quays and to admire the merchandise that has traveled from Arabia, India and perhaps even from Cathay [China]. (Epistle 11)

As soon as he arrived, Paul was anxious to make contact with the Christians of Puteoli, who welcomed him with signs of the greatest affection and respect. He then departed again on foot for Rome, at first by the Via Consularis, crossing the plains of Campania. After a nineteen mile walk, he reached Capua, which is famous for its amphi-theater, the largest in the empire after the Colosseum in Rome, and also for its statue of Venus, Hannibal, and the revolt of the slaves.

The road joined there with the Via Appia, the Appian Way, built in 312 B.C. during the war against the Samnites. It was marked with milestones and every forty feet there was a bench on which to rest. Every nineteen miles or so, a *mansio*, or relay post, accommodated travelers; there one could hire horses and all sorts of vehicles for the well-to-do or government officials. From Capua it is twenty-five miles to Sinuessa and Mount Massicus, which produced wines that were celebrated in song by Virgil and Horace. And

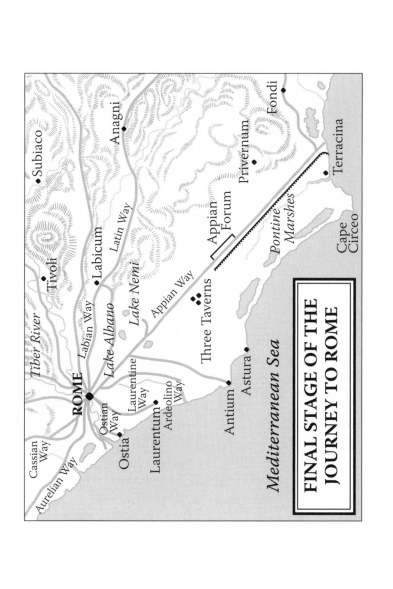

FINAL STAGE OF THE JOURNEY TO ROME

suddenly, at a turn in the road, they were greeted with a splendid view of the Gulf of Gaeta. The whole coastline was sprinkled with villas occupied by wealthy Romans.

They stopped at Formiae, one of the most beautiful cities in Italy. That was the location of Cicero's villa, Formianum, and there he was assassinated by Mark Antony's henchmen, on the seventh day before the Ides of December 711 (or December 7, 63 B.C. by our reckoning). Around midday the travelers reached Fondi and from there crossed the mountain pass of Latudae. At that spot Quintus Fabius Maximus stopped Hannibal in his march toward Rome. A long canal had been dug that allowed the travelers to be transported through the Pontine Marshes, as Strabo tells us, without fatigue and protected from heat and mosquitoes and therefore from malaria.

Paul and his companions disembarked at the Forum Appii. Appius had established a marketplace for the people of the vicinity while he was building the road that bears his name. Horace spent the night there with Maecenas and Virgil, en route to Brindisi, for the purpose of reconciling Augustus Caesar and Mark Antony. He found the drinking water execrable and the place swarming with juggling crooks and swindling innkeepers.

There, thirty-seven miles from Rome, Paul met some Christians from the city, a sign that his coming was awaited. At the following stop, the Tres Tabernae, or the Three Taverns, another delegation, perhaps more important and more official, was waiting for him. "On seeing them Paul thanked God and took courage" (Acts 28:15).

They passed Bovillae, which is nine miles from the Eternal City. At that spot the road leads straight ahead into the plain, lined on either side with magnificent tombs in the middle of flowering gardens. They could see the enormous Etruscan rotundas, the graceful miniature replicas of Greek

temples, and Roman sepulchers of all sorts, like that of
Cecilia Metella, or the massive, very simple sarcophagus
of Scipio.

They crossed the little river Almo and made their way
into the capital city by the Porta Capena, passing the ramparts that were thought to have been built by Servius Tullius. That was the gate through which conquering generals
and victorious Caesars entered in triumph, crowned with
laurels, ascending to the Capitol in the splendor of purple
garments and shining weapons, preceded by bronze breastplates and pikes, with the captives and the spoils of war
following after.

To the left, in the valley between the Aventine and Palatine hills, loomed the Circus Maximus, where the applause
of the crowd annoyed the emperor Caracalla so much
that he sent soldiers to disperse the spectators. Our travelers reached the Via Sacra, the Sacred Way that descends
toward the Sacer Clivus [Sacred Slope], on which stood
the gilded landmark that was the point of departure for all
the distances in the Roman world. All roads led to Rome,
to the Forum Romanum, and therefore to the heart of the
known world.

Not far from there Paul perhaps noticed the hundred
steps leading up to the Capitolium, toward the temple of
Jupiter Tonans, which was adorned with all sorts of finery
and resplendent with the spoils brought back from everywhere in the ancient world. And on the left he could see the
Palatine, which gave its name to the "palace" that Caesar
had built on the hill where the modest hut of Romulus,
with its thatch roof, was preserved. Pompey's theater was
located near the Campus Martius, the first Roman theater
to be built of stone. And there the Mausoleum of
Augustus and the Pantheon of Agrippa, still brand new;
the bronze from the dome can still be seen today in the

form of the baldachin in St. Peter's Basilica.

The barracks of the Praetorian Guard had been situated by Tiberius to the northeast of the city. A detachment of praetorians was quartered near the Palace. That is where the very patient centurion Julius brought Paul, who had surely become his friend; he presented him to the prefect of the Praetorian Guard, a man by the name of Afranius Burrus. Other scholars think that he was entrusted to the Princeps Peregrinorum, the commander of the foreign legionaries, at his headquarters on the Caelian Hill or on the Tarquinian field, on the Viminal Hill.

Paul had written, "I must also see Rome" (Acts 19:21). Now he was in Rome in the month of March or April, A.D. 61.

The city built along the two banks of the Tiber extended over the famous seven hills that marked a circumference of around eleven miles. It contained several beautiful areas, such as the Forum and the Campus Martius ["Field of Mars"], but the streets were dirty, narrow, veritable labyrinths, dangerous at night, and flanked by tall, overpopulated buildings, the insulae, very unhealthy lodgings. The city counted one million inhabitants (Carcopino), a large number of them slaves, who did all the work. There was no "middle class", only a small minority of very well-to-do individuals and their clients, and then a multitude of poor or very poor citizens who demanded from their masters bread and games: *panem et circenses.*

They lived mainly on the sportula, a gift of money or foodstuffs that the patron made to his clients who, every day, from early morning on, sought to come see him, to praise him, to serve him, to make a good impression, to arouse his generosity and munificence. In addition there was a throng of jugglers, soldiers of fortune, and speculators, parasites, impostors, mystagogues, enchantresses, and ladies of the night.

The Rome of that day presented a stupefying mixture of pride and lowliness, luxury and misery, superstition, shameless materialism, cruelty, contempt for mankind, sorcery—not to mention the atrocious practices of ritual crime, such as the sorceress who, disheveled and shrieking, scratched at the ground with her nails and buried an infant alive, so as to use the body later for diabolical incantations and to extract from its blood a love potion.

The Jews in Rome

Starting in the year 63 B.C., when Pompey conquered Palestine, several thousand Jews were deported to Rome as slaves. Others came as travelers or businessmen. They lived in the Ghetto, to the east of the Tiber. Julius Caesar, whom they had helped in his rise to power, granted them certain privileges. Augustus allowed them to practice their religion freely and even to benefit from a share in the distribution of grain. They constituted, however, a troublesome element, and in the year 19 B.C. Tiberius banished them from Rome and deported several thousands of them to the sulfur mines of Sardinia.

In the year A.D. 52 they were banished again by order of the emperor Claudius, not only from Rome but from the whole Italian peninsula. They soon returned and formed an industrious and prosperous community served by a dozen synagogues. Very quickly they crossed the Tiber over the bridge built by Fabricius one hundred years previously. The poet Martial, who lived on the Via Pirus, on the Quirinal, complained that he could not sleep because of the noise made by the Jewish peddlers. Juvenal, for his part, tells us about Jewish fortune-tellers who interpreted dreams for a little bit of money. They were even seen frequenting the public baths, although they were not foolish enough to reveal in that way their Jewish identity. Horace, Cicero, Perseus, and Tacitus made fun of them. But certain high-ranking Roman personages converted to Judaism, for instance, Poppaea, the mistress and then the wife of Nero. Nero's favorite actor, Aliturus, was Jewish.

Only three days after his arrival, Paul (who was incessantly in motion) sent for the leaders of the community. When they had gathered, he told them,

> Brethren, though I had done nothing against the people or the customs of our fathers, yet I was delivered [as a] prisoner from Jerusalem into the hands of the Romans. When they had examined me, they wished to set me at liberty, because there was no reason for the death penalty in my case. But when the Jews objected, I was compelled to appeal to Caesar.... For this reason therefore I have asked to see you and speak with you, since it is because of the hope of Israel that I am bound with this chain. (Acts 28:17–20)

They answered him, "We have received no letters from Judea about you.... But we desire to hear from you what your views are; for with regard to this sect we know that everywhere it is spoken against" (28:21–22).

After setting a date with him, they came to visit him in greater numbers. Paul forcefully presented to them his testimony about the Kingdom of God, seeking to persuade them by the Law of Moses and the Prophets of the truth about Jesus; the conversation lasted from morning till evening.

> And some were convinced by what he said, while others disbelieved. So, as they disagreed among themselves, they departed, after Paul had made one statement: "The Holy Spirit was right in saying to your fathers through Isaiah the prophet: 'Go to this people, and say, You shall indeed hear but never understand.... For this people's heart has

grown dull....' Let it be known to you then that this salvation of God has been sent to the Gentiles; they will listen." (28:24–28)

Paul stayed for two whole years in lodgings that he had rented. He welcomed all who came to visit him, teaching about the Kingdom of God freely while he was being watched closely, *custodia militaris*, but not under house arrest.

12

Paul Imprisoned in Rome

Julius Caesar ordered the construction of the Saepta Julia, a voting station where the citizens voted in "centuries". In one of these rooms, Paul is said to have been guarded under constant watch for a short time. On that site today stands the church of Santa Maria in Via Lata, which was built during the reign of Pope Sergius in the eighth century and rebuilt in 1485 by Innocent VIII. But the Acts of the Apostles tell us about lodgings where Paul welcomed all "who came to him" (28:23). A not very reliable tradition situates these lodgings at the place occupied today by the little church of San Paolo alla Regola, near the Sixtus Bridge and the Balbus theater.

Paul, as a prisoner, was attached at the right wrist by a long, light chain to the left wrist of a praetorian guard. Flavius Josephus notes that Tiberius had Agrippa thrown into prison. Antonia, the daughter of the future emperor Claudius, bribed the prefect of the praetor Macro to have Agrippa placed under the guard of a benevolent centurion and to grant him the privilege of taking his meals with his hands free. Perhaps Paul enjoyed the same privileges. He was chained to one soldier by day and to two by night—for two years! Many guards had the opportunity to observe Paul's life and activity, whether alone or with visitors. We can imagine that at certain points these guards got into discussions with this enigmatic figure who spoke about a Savior named Christ and that they talked about it afterward with their companions in the guardroom. Is there any doubt that he converted several or even a great number of them? This is how we should understand what Paul says in the Letter to the Philippians: "I want you to know, brethren, that what has happened to me has really served to advance the gospel, so that it has become known throughout the whole praetorian guard and to all the rest that my imprisonment is for Christ" (Phil 1:12–13).

It was not only the soldiers; at a higher level, in the imperial palace, the influence of Paul made itself felt also. We find traces of this later in the same letter: "All the saints greet you, especially those of Caesar's household" (4:22).

At liberty but under surveillance, Paul had enough independence to act that "most of the brethren have been made confident in the Lord because of my imprisonment, and are much more bold to speak the word of God without fear" (1:14). It is clear that his influence extended well into the city.

Some of those brethren preached the gospel of Christ for the purest of motives, but others, in contrast, "preach[ed] Christ from envy and rivalry" (1:15). Paul didn't mind: "What then? Only that in every way, whether in pretense or in truth, Christ is proclaimed" (1:18).

Luke, his faithful companion, was with Paul in Rome. That gave him the opportunity and the time to gather the information necessary for the composition of his Gospel and Acts. Paul had with him also Timothy, his beloved "child in the faith" (1 Tim 1:2), and Aristarchus from Thessalonica, who had risked his life for Paul in Ephesus and had been, along with Luke, his traveling companion from Caesarea to Rome. Tychicus from Ephesus was with him also for a time, as was Epaphroditus from Philippi; Mark, who had regained Paul's confidence; Demas, who would later abandon him; Jesus Justus, a man "of the circumcision",

Book of Life

THE WORLD OF SAINT PAUL

who was a big help to Paul; Onesimus, the runaway slave;
Epaenetus, Ampliatus, Stachys, Tryphaena and Tryphosa,
Aquila and Prisca, and his dear Persis and Maria, who had
"worked hard" for the Church (See Rom 1–16). Their
names are inscribed in the Book of Life!

At that moment Christianity was still only an obscure
sect that united a small number of believers, a "miserable
superstition", as Tacitus said. Nevertheless, that superstition was on the way to conquering the world. How many
works by Greek or Roman writers have vanished! And of
those that have come down to us, how many still have any
influence? Who, for example, still reads Seneca? Annaeus
Seneca, a Spaniard, was exiled to Corsica by Messalinus in
A.D. 41 because he had committed adultery with Julia, the
daughter of Germanicus. Called back in 49, he became the
tutor of Nero, which made him then and for a long time
to come the greatest statesman of the Roman world. He
committed suicide at Nero's orders in the year 65.

In contrast, the four Gospels, Acts, the letters of Paul,
in short, the books of the New Testament, are still today a
source of spiritual life for hundreds of millions of believers,
translated into all the languages of the world, in the past,
at present, and until the Last Judgment.

Letter to the Philippians

Since we have just cited this letter several times, this may
be the place to discuss it, although the date of its composition is much disputed. Some scholars date it to Ephesus
in 56, while others prefer to assign it instead to late 62 or
early 63. We have no intention whatsoever in this book of
participating in that controversy.

When the Christians of Philippi learned that Paul was
in prison in Rome, they organized a collection that they

entrusted to Epaphroditus to comfort the apostle who had
brought them the gospel of Jesus Christ.

When his mission was accomplished, Epaphroditus
stayed with Paul, became his companion, and worked so
hard in the Lord's vineyard that he fell sick and almost
died: "But God had mercy on him" (Phil 2:27).

The Letter to the Philippians is a very personal letter that
must be read and reread; it was inspired by gratitude toward
a Church that returned the favor that Paul had done for
it at the start of the preaching of the gospel. "I thank my
God in all my remembrance of you...making my prayer
with joy, thankful for your partnership in the gospel from
the first day until now. And I am sure that he who began
a good work in you will bring it to completion at the day
of Jesus Christ" (1:3–6).

Paul goes on to explain the significance that his captivity
may have for the benefit of his correspondents (see 1:12–30)
and calls them to practice unity and obedience like those
of Christ (see 2:1–11).

> Therefore, my beloved, as you have always obeyed, so now,
> not only as in my presence but much more in my absence,
> work out your own salvation with fear and trembling....Do
> all things without grumbling or questioning, that you
> may be blameless and innocent, children of God without
> blemish in the midst of a crooked and perverse generation,
> among whom you shine as lights in the world, holding fast
> the word of life. (2:12, 14–16)

These passages are followed by an announcement of the
arrival in Philippi of Timothy and Epaphroditus, and then
two expressions of farewell, one summarizing Paul's career,
the other consisting of an exhortation and thanksgiving:
"Finally, brethren, whatever is true, whatever is honor-
able, whatever is just, whatever is pure, whatever is lovely,

whatever is gracious, if there is any excellence, if there is
anything worthy of praise, think about these things. What
you have learned and received and heard and seen in me,
do; and the God of peace will be with you" (4:8–9).

The letter ends with the salutation "Greet every saint in
Christ Jesus. The brethren who are with me greet you. All
the saints greet you, especially those of Caesar's household.
The grace of the Lord Jesus Christ be with your spirit"
(4:21–23).

The Church of Philippi continued its existence qui-
etly, without incident, and it disappeared without leaving
a trace. It attained its immortality through a magnificent
letter of thanks that it merited by its spontaneous financial
assistance.

The Letter to Philemon

While visiting Ephesus, Paul converted Philemon of Colossae to Christianity along with his wife, Appia, and their
son Archippus. They offered their house as a meeting place;
that is why Paul calls Philemon his beloved fellow worker,
Appia his sister, and Archippus his fellow soldier.

The couple had a slave named Onesimus, who ran off,
taking with him some stolen money. He eventually arrived
in Rome.

Tied with the Second and Third Letters of John, the
shortest book in the New Testament is this little letter that
Paul wrote during his captivity. It begins with the greeting
and thanksgiving that are typical of Paul's letters. Then the
author urges Philemon to be kind to his slave, whom Paul
"fathered" by converting him. Paul hopes that Philemon
will welcome Onesimus "no longer as a slave but [as] more
than a slave". He is convinced that Philemon "will do even
more than I say" (Philem 10, 16, 21). Paul no doubt was

thinking about emancipation. He is even willing to pay for any expenses that Philemon might incur.

We should recall here the fact that in Athens slavery was relatively mild, that it was forbidden to strike slaves or even to insult them, whereas in Rome the law and general prejudice made no distinction between them and beasts of burden, and they were sold on the same terms as cattle. In the houses of the great, although the dog wandered about freely, the slave who served as porter was attached to the doorjamb by a chain. Silence in the master's presence was an absolute rule, and all sorts of corporal punishment and even torture were in common use. There was only one hope for all those unfortunate souls: emancipation.

This note attests to the cordial affection and the refined tact of the apostle. Paul was by no means a social reformer traveling through the world so as to break the chains of slavery. But even for the lowliest slave who had run away from his master, he is full of fraternal love, because for him the slave, too, had been redeemed by Christ and incorporated into him.

The Letter to the Colossians

It so happened that Epaphras, the "beloved fellow servant" of Paul, came to Rome and told him the news about the situation in Phrygia, in the valley of the Lycos River, in the vicinity of Laodicea, Colossae, and Hierapolis, cities that were quite close to one another. He mentioned their faith and their great charity but did not conceal certain heretical tendencies, the products of a troubled imagination and a pursuit of illusions that were manifest in the religious practices of the Church of Colossae.

The main subject of the letter is what Paul considers a wrong interpretation of the role of Jesus, combined with

heretical ideas about the nature of the world. If the opinions
of the Colossians could be reconstructed, the exact mean-
ing of what Paul is trying to say would be clearer to us.
Unfortunately he is almost always content to make vague
allusions to their errors. Still, it is evident that they attached
great importance to the "elemental spirits", observed the
Jewish calendar, and devoted themselves to ascetical practices; they participated also in what he calls the "worship of
angels" (Col 2:8, 16–18, 21). It is not entirely clear whether
he called their opinions "philosophy" or they did. It is the
only time that this word appears in the New Testament.

From the objections that the apostle makes to his correspondents, we can deduce the following points:

1. Christ is the only agent of the creation of the world
and of universal reconciliation (see 1:15–20). In other
words, if "things... visible and invisible, whether thrones
or dominions or principalities or authorities" (1:16) existed,
they would owe their existence to Christ and consequently
they are inferior to him; therefore they should not be worshipped as though they were autonomous beings.

2. At the time of his Crucifixion, Christ made a public
spectacle of the "principalities and powers" (2:15), disarming
them and triumphing over those who rebel against God.

3. Through baptism Christians are buried then raised
again from the dead (see 2:12); they reject the teachings
about the "elemental spirits of the universe" (2:20); their
true life is "hidden with Christ in God" (3:3).

4. It is true that this life has not yet been revealed fully;
there are still "members" that are earthly. The "new man"
must be unceasingly renewed (3:10). In principle, however,
a Christian is no longer subject to the spirits.

Paul insists also on the unity of the people of God; in
his heart there is no longer "Greek and Jew, circumcised
and uncircumcised, barbarian, Scythian, slave, free man,

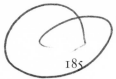

but Christ is all, and in all" (3:11). After compiling a list of faults that the Colossians should eliminate or avoid (two groups of five sins each), the apostle specifies the garments (i.e., virtues) befitting "God's chosen ones" (3:12) and then enumerates their familial duties after the manner of the Stoic philosophers.

The Letter to the Ephesians

In Colossians 4:16 Paul had written, "When this letter has been read among you, have it read also in the Church of the Laodiceans [which was only nine miles away]; and see that you read also the letter from Laodicea." He was perhaps alluding to the letter that we are discussing now, which seems to have been a circular letter to be read throughout the region: in Ephesus, Laodicea, Colossae, and maybe other neighboring cities such as Hierapolis.

The theme of the letter is set forth in the blessing and thanksgiving with which it opens. God has blessed Christians, choosing them in Christ before the foundation of the world and making known to them the mystery of his will. This mystery, which is destined to be revealed to everyone, was "a plan for the fulness of time, to unite all things in [Christ], things in heaven and things on earth" (Eph 1:10).

From now on, God has made Christ "the head over all things for the Church, which is his body, the fulness of him who fills all in all" (1:22–23). Christians are therefore seated "with him in the heavenly places in Christ Jesus" (2:6). "For by grace you have been saved through faith" (2:8).

However, whereas in the Letter to the Colossians the union of all was considered primarily in relation to the universe, here the theme is the union between Jews and Gentiles in the Church. Formerly "far off", the Gentiles have been "brought near" and have become fellow citizens with the

armor of God

saints and form part of God's temple (2:13). Thanks to the Church, the infinite wisdom of God is henceforth known, even to the principalities and powers who dwell in the heavenly places. The unity of the Church lies in the fact that her members conduct themselves according to one morality, especially in family life; for the relations between husband and wife can be compared to those that exist between Christ and the Church. This moral conduct must extend to all, for example, children and parents as well as to slaves and masters.

Paul pauses for a moment. Let's not forget that when he was writing this letter he was still in *custodia militaris* and for years, ever since Caesarea, had been attached to a soldier by a light chain. The praetorian guards often busied themselves around him; he heard everywhere the clanking of weapons and quite naturally made the transition to military language. But his weapons are the spiritual means available to the Christian.

> Therefore take [and put on] the whole *armor* of God, that you may be able to withstand in the evil day, and having done all, to stand. Stand, therefore, having fastened the *belt* of truth around your waist, and having put on the *breastplate* of righteousness, and having shod your feet with the equipment of the gospel of peace; besides all these, taking the *shield* of faith, with which you can quench all the flaming *darts* of the Evil One. And take the *helmet* of salvation, and the *sword* of the Spirit, which is the word of God.... Keep alert with all perseverance, making supplication for all the saints, and also for me, that utterance may be given me in opening my mouth boldly to proclaim the mystery of the gospel, for which I am an ambassador in chains. (6:13–20; italics added)

And the apostle concludes: "Grace be with all who love our Lord Jesus Christ with love undying" (6:24).

13

Final Journeys, Second Captivity, Martyrdom

Freed of his chains after two years of captivity, Paul was ready to go wherever the Lord would lead him. Some years previously he had expressed the desire to visit Spain. Clement of Rome, around the year 95, wrote to the Corinthians that Paul had preached "to the ends of the Occident". Now for a Roman at the time we are dealing with, the Iberian Peninsula was at the Western limits of the world.

It seems instead that Paul, perhaps impelled by the Spirit, traveled to his favorite field of apostolate, to Asia Minor and Greece. He began with Crete and left Titus there in charge of the churches (see Tit 1:5). They still existed in the second century because at that time Dionysius of Corinth wrote a letter to the Christians of Crete.

At Ephesus Paul put an end to the quarrels that were troubling that church by replacing Hymenaeus, Philetus, and Alexander with Timothy. While in prison, Paul had promised the Philippians that he would come soon to pay them a visit, and it is quite likely that he kept his promise after that visit to Ephesus.

He went next to Corinth and from there sent Artemas to replace Titus, who was asked to join Paul at Nicopolis, where the latter counted on spending the winter. From Lechaeum, the western port of Corinth, Paul set sail for Nicopolis, "City of Victory", the capital of Epirus. It had been founded by Augustus to commemorate the great naval victory at Actium over Mark Antony and Cleopatra in September A.D. 31, which made him the master of the Roman world.

Nicopolis was a Roman colony, a free city, adorned with splendid monuments erected by foreign princes to flatter Augustus. Herod the Great had particularly distinguished himself by contributing statues and temples of great beauty.

From Nicopolis, Paul visited Epirus as well as Illyria and also Dalmatia; otherwise he would not have sent Titus (see 2 Tim 4:10). After that we find him in Troas, as the guest of Carpus, to whom he entrusted his cloak, his books, and especially his parchments (Greek: *malista*; Latin: *membrana*) (see 2 Tim 4:13). Probably that was where he was arrested and then brought to Ephesus to be judged by the proconsul Quintus Marcius Barea Soranus. Ignatius, the bishop of Antioch in Syria, compared himself in the year 150 to Paul, who, like him, had been sent from Ephesus to Rome to undergo martyrdom. It is quite possible that Paul once again, as a Roman citizen, had appealed to Caesar. Or perhaps Barea Soranus, unwilling to execute the apostle, sent him to Nero. Soranus could not escape the indiscriminate rage of Nero; the latter had him executed in Rome in the year 66.

From Ephesus, the convoy that included Paul stopped at Miletus, where Trophimus, who had become ill, was entrusted to friends. In Corinth Erastus bid him farewell. In Lechaeum they embarked for Aulon in Illyria and, crossing the strait, arrived in Brindisi. From there, by the Via Appia, they reached Rome.

First Letter to Timothy

During that voyage, perhaps while he was in Macedonia, Paul wrote the First Letter to Timothy. This is one of what are usually called the pastoral letters. This name, however, goes back only to the eighteenth century. The Church has always held that Paul is the author of these pastoral letters. However, in the nineteenth century and up to this day, some liberal and rationalist scholars have tried to refute this attribution. They argue that the kind of hierarchy, the notion of the apostolic succession, of tradition that are found in these letters could not have emerged at such an early stage in the history of the Church. The Pontifical Biblical Commission has responded that these objections are based on a priori attitudes as to how and when the Church structures came to be established. At that time Timothy was in Ephesus, responsible for the Christian community. According to the information that we can derive from the letter, it seems that this community, although firmly established, was experiencing the difficulties that were typical in early Christian times. The pagan milieu in which it lived, the heterodox teachings propagated by some self-styled disciples, the hostility of the Jews, and instances of dissolute living, threatened the stability of the young Church.

Paul exhorts Timothy to make sure that true doctrine is taught and to encourage the believers to live the Christian life fervently. He must be vigilant, so as to keep intact the deposit of faith and to devote himself to instructing the faithful; he must know also how to conduct himself in the house of God, which is the Church of God, the pillar and bulwark of the truth (see 1 Tim 3:15). False teachings must be rejected forcefully, and he recommends that they not occupy themselves "with myths and endless genealogies which promote speculations rather than the divine training that is in faith" (1:4).

He must vigilantly exercise his authority, but he must also fight the good fight of the faith and win the eternal life to which he has been called and for which he made that fine profession of faith before a large number of witnesses (see 6:12). The practice of virtue (which the ministers must practice in an exemplary manner) must go hand in hand with keeping the faith and a clear conscience. "By rejecting conscience, certain persons have made shipwreck of their faith" (1:19).

Timothy is also charged with improving the management of the church by making sure that the deacons are "serious, not double-tongued" [i.e., without duplicity] (3:8). The letter lists also the virtues that can be expected of bishops, priests, deacons, and widows. Timothy must also consider impartially any accusation against an "elder", provided that it is supported by two or three witnesses (see 5:19).

The Letter to Titus

Titus had been sent to Crete "that you might amend what was defective, and appoint elders in every town" (Tit 1:5).

It was a difficult field of action because, as the proverb says, "The Kretans, the Kappadocians and the Kilikians [Cilicians] are the three worst K's, *tria kappa kaka*, in the [ancient] world."

The Cretans were first-rate liars, and it was said that they owed their reputation to the fact that they claimed that Zeus, the supreme god, had died and was buried on their island.

Plutarch declares that the Cretans were "as interested in money as bees are in their hive". In his poem "The Oracles", Epimenides, in the sixth century B.C., himself a Cretan, depicts Cretans as inveterate liars, vicious animals, and lazy gluttons. Callimachus repeats the formula in his "Hymn to Zeus"; Paul does the same and adds, "This testimony is true."

It seems obvious that, in these circumstances, remarkable disciples were needed to found the church of Crete and to defend it against the enemy. For this difficult task Paul chose Titus.

Titus, the son of Gentiles, was probably baptized by Paul, judging by the affection that the latter has for him: "Titus, my true child in a common faith" (1:4). He accompanied Paul and Barnabas to Jerusalem at the time of the first council. He is not mentioned in Acts, but we know that at the end of the third missionary journey he was sent to Corinth for two delicate missions, first to deliver a letter, and second to organize a collection and to bring back a second letter.

As in the First Letter to Timothy, the apostle offers his advice about organizing the community properly; he underscores the need to protect the flock from specious ideas that certain individuals were beginning to propagate. He insists on the importance of a good choice of very capable persons for the ministry of evangelization, especially the elders. They must be firm in their faith and morally irreproachable (see 1:5–9). The other Christians, too—old men, young and older women, young people, and slaves—must live a blameless life that is completely in keeping with the faith that they profess so as to edify the pagans and especially the authorities (see 3:1–2).

In order to defend the truth, Titus has to make every effort to silence those "many insubordinate men... [who] are upsetting whole families" (1:10–11). He must not intervene in quarrels and disputes concerning the Law. First and foremost he must be "a model of good deeds, and in your teaching show integrity, gravity, and sound speech that cannot be censured, so that an opponent may be put to shame, having nothing evil to say of us" (2:7–8).

Paul before His Judges

"I appeal to Caesar", Paul had protested. "You have appealed to Caesar; to Caesar you shall go", Festus had replied (Acts 25:11–12). At Ephesus he repeated that appeal. Let us see now which Caesar Paul was going to meet in hopes of receiving an impartial judgment.

Gnaeus Domitius Ahenobarbus (Barbarossa, "Red-beard"!), was a vicious man who married Agrippina, the dissolute sister of Caligula. One cynic had remarked, "Nothing will come of that union but detestable deeds and danger for the public welfare." A real prophet! Agrippina gave birth to a boy on December 15, A.D. 31, who was named Lucius. She reportedly consulted soothsayers about him; they predicted that the young child would one day be emperor and assassinate his mother. Her response? "Let him kill me, provided that he reigns!"

The sexual debauchery of Agrippina was such that Caligula found himself compelled to banish her from Rome. As for her husband, he died of his excesses three years later.

When Cassius Chaerea pierced Caligula through with his sword, Agrippina was called back from exile. The widow married the advocate Cassius Capiena and, upon the latter's death, became the fourth wife of the emperor Claudius in the year 49. On February 25, A.D. 50, he declared Lucius his adopted son and gave him the name of Nero Claudius Caesar Drusus Germanicus. In early 53, Claudius married the sixteen-year-old Nero to his daughter Octavia, who was then thirteen.

Claudius, a weak ruler and outwitted by his new wife, had designated Nero as his successor. A dish of mushrooms specially seasoned by Agrippina was enough to bring about the ascent of the young prince to the throne, since the emperor was dead at this point. Nero himself pronounced the funeral oration, composed by Seneca, on the occasion of the grandiose funeral ceremonies.

Nero's beginnings did not augur a criminal future; he was even cultivated, to some extent. Flanked by honest Burrus and the wise Seneca, his governor and minister, surrounded by universal admiration, the new master of Rome apparently was somewhat inclined to win sympathy and popularity by the usual methods: displays of largess, munificence, a fondness for festivals, and favors granted at his good pleasure. He had a shady, deceitful character, however, and was very jealous of his power and inebriated by his omnipotence; as long as his mother was alive he was champing at the bit, feigning and dissembling, consumed by the need for applause, eager for praise, confusing the satisfaction of the stupidest vanity with a true desire for glory, which is incommensurate with it.

He wrote verses and sang them, accompanying himself on the zither. He would go onstage as an actor so as to win acclaim for his talents and his singing voice. He would become a chariot driver; during a tour of Greece he would aspire to the crowns reserved from antiquity for accomplishments in the theaters of Achaea, expecting to be applauded again in the Roman theaters as he sang about the conflagration of Troy while almost all of Rome was burning.

But even before he spilled blood, there were terrible signs of the demons that would later drive that *energoumenos*, or "possessed man", as they used to say in Greek, to commit major crimes.

Agrippina was ambitious. She wanted to share the throne with her son. But there were dangerous rivals: since Lucian Silanus, the great-grandson of Caesar Augustus, was one of them, he was eliminated. His brother Junius—the proconsul of the province of Asia who had no political ambition whatsoever—was poisoned during a very hospitable banquet. Nero's half brother, Britannicus, son of Claudius and Messalina, a fourteen-year-old boy, also had a claim to the throne. During a pleasant family reunion he died, a victim of the same "Agrippinian" recipe.

Seneca wrote his *De Clementia* to cover up the bad impression that that crime had made.

All these deaths made Nero uneasy.

In the year 59, Nero was at Baiae, near Naples; he invited his mother, who lived in Bauli, and planned a feast in her honor. After the banquet, as she was about to depart, he took her in his arms and kissed her tenderly. Tacitus tells us that Nero's tutor, Anicetus, had received orders to take her home by boat and drown her; she was a good swimmer, however, and escaped. Anicetus was sent to Bauli again, accompanied by the commander of a navy squadron and a centurion. They slipped into Agrippina's bedroom, overpowered her, and finished her off with the sword.

Nero himself made a report to the Senate declaring that Agrippina had sent Agerinus to assassinate him and, upon learning that the plan had failed, took her own life. Nero returned to the capital, and the Romans, fooled, welcomed him joyously and offered sacrifices to the gods in the temples as a sign of gratitude. The Senate in assembly declared in the name of the city of Rome that Agrippina's death was beneficial to the city.

> "Nero is our idol," they all proclaimed aloud,
> While quietly they murmured, "He is a trifling lout."

The circus, near the Palatine Hill, caught fire, and it spread to the Caelian Hill during the night of July 18–19, A.D. 64. Neither temples nor blocks of houses nor individual dwellings were spared. The widespread calamity seemed to have started everywhere and lasted six days, then resumed when it was thought to have been warded off. Ten of the fourteen districts of the city were annihilated.

Nero, who had hastened from Antium [Anzio] upon hearing news of the disaster, opened the Campus Martius to the homeless people who were wandering about, had barracks built in his gardens for the disaster victims, and gave orders to distribute grain to the needy. But these measures failed to achieve their purpose, which was to increase the prince's popularity. For the rumor had spread that while Rome was burning, Nero had walked onto the stage of his private theater, lyre in hand, and, as Tacitus relates, "sang of the destruction of Troy, comparing present misfortunes with the calamities of antiquity." In order to deflect the infamous rumor that the conflagration was the result of his direct order, Nero looked for guilty parties and blamed the destruction of the city "on a class hated for their abominations and called Christians by the populace".

Tacitus continues:

> Accordingly, an arrest was first made of all who pleaded guilty; then, upon their information, an immense multitude was convicted, not so much of the crime of firing the city, as of hatred against mankind. Mockery of every sort was added to their deaths. Covered with the skins of beasts, they were torn by dogs and perished, or were nailed to crosses, or were doomed to the flames and burnt, to serve as a nightly illumination, when daylight had expired.
>
> Nero offered his gardens for the spectacle, and was exhibiting a show in the circus, while he mingled with the people in the dress of a charioteer or stood aloft on a car. Hence, even for criminals who deserved extreme and exemplary punishment, there arose a feeling of compassion; for it was not, as it seemed, for the public good, but to glut one man's cruelty, that they were being destroyed. (Tacitus, *Annals*, chapter 15, passim)

All this carnage took place in the first days of the month of August in A.D. 64.

Nero's gardens, inherited from his mother, Agrippina, were located on the Vatican Hill.

Sulpicius Severus informs us that the burning of Rome marked the beginning of the persecution of Christians. "Afterwards, too, their religion was prohibited by laws which were enacted; and by officially published edicts it was proclaimed unlawful to be a Christian."

The persecution swiftly spread to the provinces. Christians had to offer sacrifices officially to the emperor and to the idols and to curse the name of Christ; if they refused, they were thrown into prison or executed.

New Imprisonment in Rome

Paul had arrived from Ephesus for a new trial in the capital. He no longer enjoyed the privileges of his first incarceration but was imprisoned—perhaps, as one tradition says, in the famous Mamertine, which was built over the dungeon constructed by Servius Tullius and called the Tullianum. Sallust describes it as follows: "In the prison, when you go up a bit to the left, there is a place called the Tullianum, sunk about twelve feet into the ground. It is enclosed on all sides by walls and forms a cavern with a vault of cut stones. The filth, darkness and odor give it a hideous and terrible aspect."

Paul was compelled to follow such a severe regimen that Onesiphorus, who used to refresh him at Ephesus, could find him only after making diligent inquiries. Winter was approaching and it was so cold that Paul asked them to send him the cloak (paenula) that he had left with Carpus in Troas.

Appeals to Caesar in civil cases originating in the provinces were heard in one of the basilicas surrounding the

Forum by a delegate of the emperor. But Paul, now, was considered as a criminal, and these cases were dealt with by Nero personally.

Tiberius and Claudius had judged such matters at the Forum, but Nero, following the example of Augustus, judged them on the Palatine, in the temple of Apollo connected with the Greek and Latin libraries, the whole complex enclosed within a splendid portico. But nothing was left of the Palatine but ashes, and it is very likely that Paul was brought to the Domus Aurea, the Golden House of Nero on the Caelian and Esquiline hills.

Normally the emperor, "having powers equal to those of the gods" (Juvenal), clad in the toga made of imperial purple, presided over the session. But this was the year 67, and Nero had been in Greece, for his Grand Tour, since the spring of 66 and did not return from it until early 68. According to Clement of Rome, several "governors" delegated by the prince substituted for him.

In a lower position twelve assessors were seated. Each of them had three tablets, one marked "A" for *absolvo*, "not guilty"; another marked "C" for *condemno*, "guilty"; and finally a third with the letters "NL" for *non liquet*, adjourn for further inquiry.

After the indictment was read, Paul defended himself with his characteristic mettle, despite the difficult incarceration. "But the Lord stood by me and gave me strength to proclaim the word fully, that all the Gentiles might hear it. So I was rescued from the lion's mouth" (2 Tim 4:17). He did this so forcefully that, for the moment, he was not condemned. *Non liquet!*

"The lion is dead", the jailer might have said to Agrippa when he released him from prison at the death of Tiberius. We read in the Old Testament that Queen Esther went "before the lion" (Xerxes).

Back in prison Paul, who liked to be surrounded by people, felt lonely and very discouraged. Crescens had been sent to Galatia, Titus to Dalmatia, Tychicus to Ephesus; Trophimus was sick in Miletus. "Luke alone is with me. Get Mark and bring him with you; for he is very useful in serving me" (2 Tim 4:11). Paul sent greetings from Eubulus, Pudens, Linus, Claudia, and all the brethren. Hopefully they were able to help and comfort him in prison even though they had not dared to defend him at the tribunal.

It was during this second captivity, a few weeks before his execution, that Paul dictated his Second Letter to Timothy. It was his swan song, the expression of his last will.

Following the salutation and the thanksgiving, Paul exhorts his "beloved child" (1:2) to take his share of suffering in order to spread the gospel "in the power of God, who saved us and called us with a holy calling, not in virtue of our works but in virtue of his own purpose and the grace which he gave us in Christ Jesus" (1:8–9).

Paul continues: "Take your share of suffering as a good soldier of Christ Jesus ... as preached in my gospel, the gospel for which I am suffering and wearing chains like a criminal. But the word of God is not chained" (2:3, 8–9).

Paul warns Timothy that "all who desire to live a godly life in Christ Jesus will be persecuted.... [A]s for you, continue in what you have learned and have firmly believed, knowing from whom you learned it and how from childhood you have been acquainted with the Sacred Writings which are able to instruct you for salvation through faith" (3:12; 14–15).

Paul beseeches Timothy to be as zealous as possible in spreading and defending the holy doctrine. "For the time is coming when people will not endure sound teaching, but having itching ears they will accumulate for themselves teachers to suit their own likings.... As for you, [Timothy,]...fulfil your ministry" (4:3, 5).

Paul stops for a moment. He knows that he does not have long to live. With a sob in his voice, perhaps, he resumes his dictation, more slowly, and provides us with this moving farewell, this song of victory: "For I am already on the point of being sacrificed; The time of my departure has come. I have fought the good fight, I have finished the race, I have kept the faith. From now on there is laid up for me the crown of righteousness, which the Lord, the righteous judge, will award to me on that Day, and not only to me but also to all who have loved his appearing" (4:6–8).

At the second hearing Paul was declared guilty, sentenced to death, and returned to prison. A delay of two days was granted so that he could petition the emperor for pardon. But the latter was not in Rome and justice followed its course.

A little procession formed at the doors of the prison. A centurion headed it, followed by Paul, surrounded by guards; the executioner and his assistants lined up after them. The little troop left the city by the Via Ostiensis, passed the pointed pyramid of Caius Cestius, and continued for 1.25 miles. Paul had difficulty keeping up, but he summoned his last strength; the guards supported him when he stumbled and could not hide their astonishment at the sight of his face, which seemed to them "like that of an angel" (cf. Acts 6:15 in reference to Saint Stephen).

The fact was that Paul was no longer of this world. In the sacred silence that enveloped him, it seems that he perceived, not with his ears but with his heart, such music that whoever hears it rejects all other melodies from then on. The song came to him from a new world, and the past, for him, had disappeared.

Over the course of more than thirty years the pastor had devoted himself to his flock, which had worn him out and exhausted him. From now on he wanted to be with the One who chose him. He closed his eyes, let himself be guided, and there he discovered the other shore where his hope would cast anchor.

The escort, meanwhile, had turned onto another road leading southeast. It followed the Via Ardentina for about a mile and stopped in a gently sloping valley that was called Ad Aquas Salvias because of the curative properties of its waters. While he was divested of his tunic and scourged, Paul, who had only a few moments left to live, might have fervently recited the Kaddish, the Jewish prayer of the dead: *Yitgadal veyitkadash shemei raba b'alma divera chireutei*: "May the glory of God be praised, may his noble name be hallowed in this world which he has created, may his kingdom arrive in our days, in our lives, and in the life of all Israel. Amen. May his holy name be blessed forever."

The executioner approached and, with a rapid stroke of his sword, he carried out his duty.

Tradition relates that three fountains sprang from the three places where the head had bounced. From then on the place acquired the name Tres Fontanae, or Three Fountains. It is said that Lucida, the wife of a Christian, acquired the apostle's remains and buried them near her family's tomb. Over his grave was constructed a little building, or *memoria*, which during the reign of Pope Anacletus became a chapel, a place of recollection and prayer.

The first Christian emperor, Constantine, in the fourth century, built a church over the grave. In 388, Valentinian, Theodosius, and Arcadius enlarged the building, which was completed by Honorius. His sister Galla Placida, wife of Atawulf, king of the Goths, had the vault of the triumphal arch covered with magnificent mosaics. The basilica was adorned with twenty-four columns of purple-veined Phrygian marble originally from a pagan basilica. On the altar of confession one can read these words by the apostle Paul:

> For to me to live is Christ
> And to die is gain.
>   (Phil 1:21)

On July 23, 1838, the apostle's sarcophagus was rediscovered in the course of excavations in the basilica, encased in a double sarcophagus of marble and bronze, with the inscription:

PAULO
APOSTOLOMAR

In July of 2007, after four years of excavations, the sarcophagus of unpolished white marble was finally extricated. It measures 8'8" × 4'1" x 3'2". The sarcophagus was not opened.

Chronology of the Life of Saint Paul

A.D. 6–10   Birth of Paul at Tarsus in Cilicia.
Initial education.

Between 21   Rabbinical education in Jerusalem at the
and 25   feet of Gamaliel.
Return to Tarsus.

36   In Jerusalem. Witness to the matyrdom of
Stephen by stoning.
Conversion en route to Damascus.
Retreat to the desert and return to
Damascus (approximately three years).

Early 39   In Jerusalem. Meeting with the apostles for
two weeks.
Return to Tarsus.

44   Barnabas goes to Tarsus to find Paul and
brings him to Antioch.
Apostolate for one year.

Spring 45   First missionary journey.
to 49   Cyprus, Attaleia, Antioch of Pisidia.
Iconium, Lystra, Derbe, and return.

Late 49–   Council of Jerusalem.
early 50   Incident in Antioch.

50–53   Second missionary journey.
Philippi, Thessalonica, Beroea, Athens,
Corinth.

around 51   Wrote the First and Second Letters to the
Thessalonians.

Early 52	Paul tried before Gallio in Corinth.
Summer 53	Paul's visit to Jerusalem.
54–58	Third missionary voyage. Ephesus.
Around 56	Wrote the Letter to the Galatians.
56 or 57	Wrote the First Letter to the Corinthians.
Autumn 56	Wrote the Letter to the Philippians
57	Visit to Corinth.
Summer 57	Journey to Macedonia.
Autumn 57	Wrote the Second Letter to the Corinthians.
Spring 58 (Easter)	Stay at Philippi in Macedonia. Wrote the Letter to the Romans.
Pentecost 58	Paul arrested in Jerusalem.
58–60	Imprisonment in Caesarea. Appearance before Felix, Festus, and King Agrippa.
Autumn 60	Transfer to Rome. Storm and shipwreck. Winter on Malta. Arrival in Rome.
61–63	First captivity in Rome. Fruitful apostolate.
62	Wrote the Letter to the Colossians, the Letter to the Ephesians, Letter to Philemon.
Late 62 or early 63	Wrote the Letter to the Philippians

63	Paul set free. Voyage to Spain (?)
64–66	Journey to Asia Minor, Crete, and Macedonia.
65	Wrote the First Letter to Timothy and the Letter to Titus.
66–67	Second captivity in Rome. Wrote the Second Letter to Timothy. Martyrdom.

Bibliography

The following Bibles were consulted:

Bible de Jérusalem. Paris: Editions du Cerf, 1961. English edition: *Jerusalem Bible*. Garden City, N.Y.; London: Doubleday; Darton, Longman and Todd, 1966.

Holy Bible, Authorized King James Version.

Ignatius Bible, Revised Standard Version, Second Catholic Edition. San Francisco: Ignatius Press, 2000.

Navarre Bible, The Letters of Saint Paul with *New Vulgate Text* of Letters (Dublin: Four Court Press, 2003).

New American Bible. 1970; 4th ed., 1994.

Nouveau Testament Crampon, Traduction Crampon révisée par Fr. Bernard-Marie. Paris: Pierre Téqui éditeur, 2004.

Nouveau Testament Interlinéaire Grec/Français, avec Traduction Oecuménique de la Bible (TOB), 1993.

Other Reference Works

Carrez, Maurice, and François Morel. *Dictionnaire grec-français du Nouveau Testament*, format de poche. 4th ed. Geneva: Pierrefitte, Labor et Fides – Société biblique française, 1989.

Carrez, Maurice. *Grammaire grecque du Nouveau Testament*. 5th ed. Geneva: Pierrefitte, Labor et Fides – Société biblique française, 1989.

Cary, M., ed. *The Oxford Classical Dictionary*. Oxford: Clarendon Press, 1957; new edition, 2003.

Leclant, J., ed. *Dictionnaire de l'Antiquité*. Paris: PUF, 2005.

Léon-Dufour, X. *Dictionnaire du Nouveau Testament*. Paris: Seuil, Livre de Vie, 1996.

Secondary Literature

ACFEB. *Les Actes des Apôtres: Histoire, Récit, Théologie*; XXe Congrès de l'Association Catholique française pour l'étude de la Bible. Edited by M. Berber. Angers, 2003. Paris: Cerf, Lectio Divina 199, 2005.

Aymard, J. and J. Auboyer. *L'Orient et la Grèce antique*. Volume 1. *L'Histoire des Civilisations*. Paris: PUF, 1953.

André, J. M., and F. M. Baslez. *Voyager dans l'Antiquité*. Paris: Fayard, 1995.

Baslez, F. M. *Saint Paul*. New ed. Paris: Fayard, 1999.

Becker, Jürgen. *Paul: Apostle to the Gentiles*. Louisville, Ky.: Westminster/John Knox, 1993.

Bevan, E. R., and C. Singer, eds. *The Legacy of Israel*. Oxford: Clarendon Press, 1928.

Blech, Rabbi Benjamin. *Understanding Judaism*. New York: Alpha, Penguin Group, 2003.

Bonsirven, J. *Le Judaïsme palestinien au temps de Jésus-Christ*. Paris, 1935.

Carcopino, J. *La Vie quotidienne à Rome à l'apogée de l'Empire*. Paris: Hachette, 1974.

Colson, J. *Paul Apôtre Martyr*. Paris: Seuil, 1971.

Daniel-Rops, Henri. *Saint Paul, conquérant du Christ*. Paris, 1952. English edition: *St. Paul, Apostle of Nations*. Translated by Jex Martin. Chicago: Fides Publishers Association, 1953.

Decaux, A. *L'Avorton de Dieu: Une vie de saint Paul*. Paris: Perrin-DDB, Collection Tempus, 2003.

Festugière, A. J. *Le monde gréco-romain au temps de Notre Seigneur*; Tome I, *Le cadre temporel*; Tome II, *Le milieu spirituel*. Paris, 1938.

Finley, M. I. *Aspects of Antiquity: Discoveries and Controversies*. Hammondsworth, Middlesex: Penguin Books, 1977.

Freely, John. *The Western Shores of Turkey*. London: John Murray, 1988.

Geoltrain, P., ed. *Aux Origines du Christianisme*. Paris: Gallimard, Folio-Histoire, 2000.

Grant, Michael. *The Rise of the Greeks*. New York: Charles Scribner's Sons, 1987.

Holzner, Joseph. *Paul of Tarsus*. Translated from German by Rev. Frederic C. Eckhoff. St. Louis, Mo., and London: B. Herder Book Company, 1944.

Landels, J. G. *Engineering in the Ancient World*. See especially chapter 6, "Ships and Sea Transport". Berkeley and Los Angeles: California University Press, 1978.

Légasse, S. *Paul Apôtre*. Québec-Paris: Fides-Cerf, 2000.

Marguerat, D. *La première Histoire du Christianisme: Les Actes des Apôtres*. Paris: Cerf, Lectio Divina 180, 1999.

Metzger, H. *Les routes de saint Paul dans l'Orient grec*. Neuchâtel-Paris: Cahiers d'archéologie Biblique, no. 4, 1954.

Morton, Henry Vollam. *In the Steps of Saint Paul.* New York: Dodd, Mead and Company, 1936.

Peters, F. E. *The Harvest of Hellenism.* New York: Simon and Schuster, 1970.

Pomey, P., ed. *La navigation dans l'Antiquité.* Aix-en-Provence: EdiSud, 1997.

Ramsay, W. M. *The Cities of St. Paul: Their Influence on His Life and Thought.* London, 1907.

Reynier, C. *Paul de Tarse en Méditerranée: Recherche autour de la navigation dans l'Antiquité (Ac 27-28, 16).* Paris: Cerf, Lectio Divina, 2006.

Ricciotti, Giuseppe. *Paul the Apostle.* Translated by Alba I. Zizzamia. Milwaukee: Bruce Publishing, 1953.

Rolland, Ph. *Et le Verbe s'est fait chair: Introduction au Nouveau Testament.* Paris: Presse de la Renaissance, 2005.

Rose, J. H. *The Mediterranean in the Ancient World.* Cambridge: Cambridge University Press, 1933.

Saffrey, H. D. *Paul à Ephèse, patrie d'Artémis.* Paris: Monde de la Bible, no. 57, 1989.

Schmidt, J. *Vie et Mort des esclaves dans la Rome antique.* Paris: Alban Michel, 1973.

Tresmontant, C. *St Paul et le Mystère du Christ.* Paris: Seuil, 1956.

Vasco, J.-L. *En Méditerranée, avec l'Apôtre Paul.* Paris: Cerf, 1972.